The
Cultural
GUTTER

by Carol Borden, Ian Driscoll, Jim Munroe,
James Schellenberg and Chris Szego

Acknowledgements

James would like to thank Fiona Scannell, Dave Switzer and Jared Penner

Ian would like to thank the casts and crews of:
>The Drunken Master Revue,
>The Dead Sleep Easy,
>The Mayfair Theatre,
>The Cultural Gutter,
and Martin Kove,
for everything cinematic.
and
Sonja VanDieen,
for everything else.

Chris would like to thank everyone in the Gutter for inviting her to the party, Anne Smith for the casting game, and the Evil Overlord for being so very, very amazing. But most of all, she'd like to thank the hundreds of writers and millions of readers who make Romance such a vibrant genre.

Carol would like to thank Kathy Borden, alex macfadyen, Steven Flusty and her colleagues at the Gutter.

Jim would like to thank Bert Archer, Guy Leshinski and Cory Doctorow

The Cultural Gutter would like to thank EJ Lee, Drew Davidson and everyone at ETC Press for all their hard work and patience.

The Cultural Gutter gratefully acknowledges the support of the Canada Council for the Arts in providing an operational grant that keeps our website going.

Foreword

Drew Davidson

The Cultural Gutter (http://theculturalgutter.com/) is a great example of how wonderful the web can be. As with most things on the web, it was a site that I found through various and sundry links and recommendations from other places. It's full of insightful articles on the art and craft found in our popular culture. And it was far enough along in its history, that I got to enjoy digging into their archive of past articles and relishing the discovery of a new site full of great content to read. The editors focus their critical eyes on science fiction, comics, romance, movies and games. And every Thursday they post a new article on one of these topics, so it has become a regular visit for me each week.

The Cultural Gutter covers topics that resonate with the focus of ETC Press on issues revolving around entertainment technologies and how they can are applied across a variety of fields. With this in mind, ETC Press worked together with the Cultural Gutter editors to create this book.

Science fiction/fantasy editor James Schellenberg, comics editor and publisher Carol Borden, romance editor Chris Szego, screen editor Ian Driscoll and founding editor and former games editor Jim Munroe, each chose ten of their favorite articles to share. And then ETC Alum, Eun Jung Lee, designed information graphics to introduce each section, as well as specific interpretative graphics for ten of the articles.

The resulting book is a great introduction to the Cultural Gutter, and serves as the tip of the iceberg. Hopefully, it will entice you into visiting the website to enjoy the thoughtful discussion around the wonderfully entertaining world of popular culture.

As they quote Oscar Wilde on their site, "We are all in the gutter, but some of us are looking at the stars." Enjoy!

Contents

The Cultural Gutter

COMICS _____109
Carol Borden

GAMES _____ 151
Jim Munroe

INDEX_____ 195
BIOS _____ 201

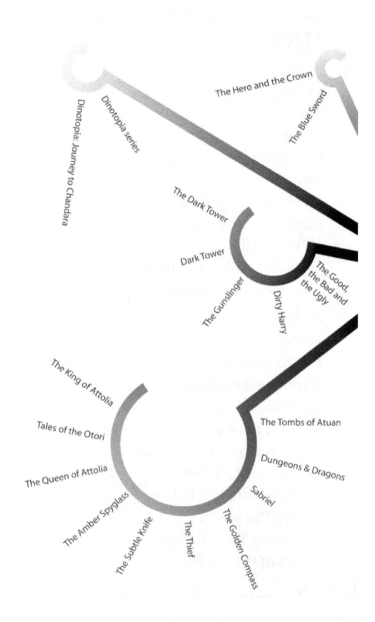

The Hero and the Crown

The Blue Sword

Dinotopia series

Dinotopia: Journey to Chandara

The Dark Tower

Dark Tower

The Good, the Bad and the Ugly

The Gunslinger

Dirty Harry

The King of Attolia

Tales of the Otori

The Tombs of Atuan

The Queen of Attolia

Dungeons & Dragons

The Amber Spyglass

Sabriel

The Subtle Knife

The Thief

The Golden Compass

SCI-FI

James Schellenberg

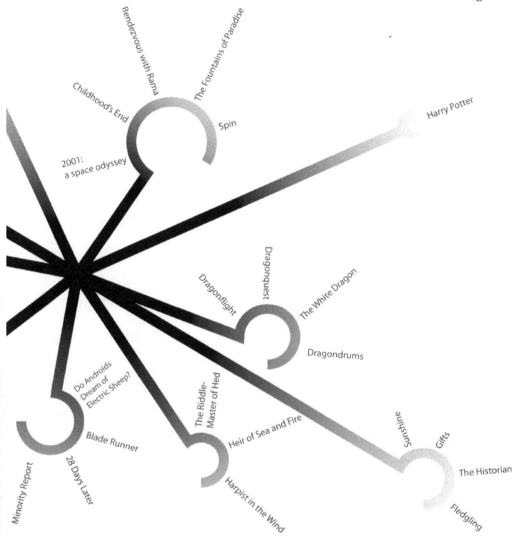

Rendezvous with Rama

The Fountains of Paradise

Childhood's End

Spin

Harry Potter

2001:
a space odyssey

Dragonquest

Dragonflight

The White Dragon

Dragondrums

Do Androids
Dream of
Electric Sheep?

The Riddle-
Master of Hed

Heir of Sea and Fire

Sunshine

Gifts

Blade Runner

The Historian

Minority Report

28 Days Later

Harpist in the Wind

Fledgling

Time Frame

Old   New

The Cultural Gutter

An Engineer and a Dreamer

I wrote this piece a few weeks after Clarke's death in March 2008.

Sad news: Arthur C. Clarke, science fiction writer and inventor/ scientist, died recently—at the age of 90, he had a full life, but it's still a great loss. To mark his passing, I picked up my favourite of his books, *Childhood's End*, and gave it a re-read. Some of his other accomplishments, like his work on *2001: a space odyssey*, might be more famous, but *Childhood's End* has always hit me hardest.

Childhood's End is about alien invasion, but like most of Clarke's work, this is not a standard-issue form of the stereotype, and it's not an invasion at all. The aliens basically show up and fix everything about human society, but they refuse to show us what they look like for fifty years. Altruistic... and sneaky? What are they waiting for? Could they have ulterior motives of some kind? The title of the book certainly seems ominous.

I was struck this time around by how weird this book is. For one thing, it's got a massively broken narrative structure. The first third of the book is a mish-mash; the ostensible protagonist—the UN Secretary General—disappears after this point, and the identity of the next leading character is not immediately obvious when the new segment starts. *2001* also has a famously broken-up timeline, and I think it's for the same reason. Clarke is trying to operate on a more-than-human time scale—the first third of *Childhood's End* covers that fifty-year period where the aliens conceal themselves—and regular humans tend to get lost in the shuffle. Likewise, *2001* jumped ahead, in that case by millennia. The ideas behind the story in *Childhood's End* tend to militate against human-scale narrative as well, as I'll explain in a minute.

The first time I read *Childhood's End* (about twenty years ago now!), my tiny little teenager's mind was blown by the big reveal at that one-third mark: the aliens who come to visit look like demons! That was about as much as I could handle, and that's about all I remembered about the book. But that was enough to burn it into the very foundations of how I read books and judge pop culture in general. The explanation later on in the book, that the medieval imagery of devils was actually a premonition of the role of these particular aliens in the termination of childhood referred to in the title, was the fireworks on the cake, so to speak. Clarke found an image, an idea with a great amount of punch, and deployed it skilfully into a science-fiction work. That's shocking stuff when you're a youngster just figuring this kind of thing out. If Clarke could wrap up so much potent material in a "low-brow" paperback, maybe other writers could too.

The second time I read *Childhood's End*, about ten years ago, I was in a Kubrick phase, so the earlier book (*Childhood's End* came out in 1953, *2001* in 1968) seemed like a pale shadow of the themes that were reworked in the movie. Interestingly, the two seem to operate entirely on different methods. In *2001*, Clarke and Kubrick created the images and ideas that subsequently had such punch *because* they inserted themselves so firmly into the stream of cultural consciousness. The monolith, the murderous computer HAL, the psychedelic trip through space, etc. *Childhood's End* manipulated existing material.

In my latest trip through the book, I noticed most keenly the nature of the end of childhood. Our current form of humanity is, apparently, very childish; at the very least, it's incredibly small and powerless in comparison to the gigantic nature of the galaxy (a point made explicitly in the book). What might the next step in human evolution look like? What's our adult form once we grow out of childhood? *Childhood's End* presents this step as both eerie and beautiful, at once dangerous, frightening, and completely necessary. There's bound to be growing pains. And when you're talking about the entire human race going through some kind of mental puberty, your storyline might have no choice but to take the wide view. The storytelling apparatus here is clunky but it still works (as a side note, I would suggest *Spin* by Robert Charles Wilson as the book that comes closest to integrating human-scale and astronomical-scale events in a readable way; in Clarke's defense, *Spin* came out fifty years after *Childhood's End*).

Clarke wrote two other books that are worth reading: *Rendezvous with Rama*, one of the best big-dumb-object stories (a subgenre where humans explore an enormous alien artifact that's generally beyond our understanding), and *The Fountains of Paradise*, which was an odd little number that helped popularize the idea of a space elevator.

I would recommend avoiding the sequels to *2001*, since the quality falls off sharply; any books "co-written" by Clarke are also reliably bad, since, as usual for such items, the quality depends on the name of the co-writer who did most of the work.

I don't think of Clarke's books as visceral favourites, but he's still a big name for me personally—*Childhood's End* and *Dune* were the two books that turned me on to science fiction all those years ago. Clarke had an engineer's mind for detail, but used that knack in the service of a dreamer's story; the resulting wild mix sometimes tended to the cold, cerebral side, but that mix was always memorable. He'll be missed.

A Decade Later

Gurney's blog (see link below) is still going strong two years later and generated material for his new book, Imaginative Realism.

The dinosaur craze seems to be over, sorry to say. One last hurrah: *Dinotopia: Journey to Chandara*, the latest entry in the Dinotopia series, is out now. James Gurney wrote and illustrated the original 3 books in the 90s, and returns to the scene of his triumph just about ten years later. Is the magic still there?

I dunno, I was never super thrilled by dinosaurs... maybe I was too old during the 90s? I mean, I saw *Jurassic Park* just like everyone else, but images of dinosaurs don't have a visceral thrill for me like some other pop culture items might. My brain is weird that way. For example, I find vampires kinda boring, but even the lowliest zombie movie will give me nightmares for weeks. Dinosaurs fall into the former category for me.

Another odd tic of mine: I get really enthusiastic about the first work of an author and then less enthused as time wears on—and this despite the fact that they should be learning their craft and improving. I might be a novelty junkie or something. (Another possible explanation: authors have long years to work on a debut, but the follow-up has to be 12 months later, as they say).

So, when *Dinotopia: Journey to Chandara* came out earlier this year, I had two things on my mind: dinosaurs... why now? And, will Gurney have improved with age or gotten boring and repetitious?

As it turns out, the 15 years since the original *Dinotopia* have worked in Gurney's favour. At the baldest level, *Journey to Chandara* is not much more than a reworking of the earlier *Dinotopia* books. But Gurney hasn't lost his writing or painting skills. And the anti-trendiness is fine too: sure, there's an element of faded glory here, but at least it's not a bandwagon any more. What's more, the easy stuff on the topic of dinosaurs has been skimmed off, so Gurney has to work harder than ever. And that's always been the key, as far as I can tell, to making a sequel that doesn't suck. If you realize that a sequel is harder, not easier, than go ahead and give it a try. Long odds, but at least you've started off a step ahead of everyone else.

The book itself breaks down into several types of things. There is text, but it's fairly straightforward stuff. An obscure manuscript turns out to be the long-lost diary of Arthur Dennison, an explorer from the 1860s who discovered the island of Dinotopia—dinosaurs and humans have a thriving society together in friendship—and is now crossing the vast land to the mysterious city of Chandara. The small bits of text are surrounded by large-scale paintings of the flora and fauna of this wonderful land.

I was amazed by the amount of detail in the depiction of dinosaurs; for one thing, the paintings include the proper Latin name of each dinosaur. Gurney has clearly done his research—a lot of interesting and recent paleontological research gets channeled into this "fictional" world. Chandara is like an excuse to portray all of the new finds from the Gobi.

My particular favourite is a linked set of two-page spreads right near the beginning of the book. The adventure starts in a city named Waterfall City, and we're given a map of it, complete with labels for all the buildings and geographical features. So far so good, I love that stuff. Then you turn the page and you get a gorgeous two page spread that shows the city itself in action. You have to turn the page back and forth, checking to see what each item is. It was a neat effect, and, oddly, better than if the map had been an inset right next to the big blow-up.

I would highly recommend the blog that Gurney set up for the book tour associated with this latest Dinotopia entry. The blog's called Gurney Journey (also available on the Amazon page for the book) and it seems like he knows everyone in the illustration and paleontology worlds. But he doesn't seem to be much of a pretentious guy—it's all a big community of excitable creative types, which makes me a little envious. And the blog itself feels generous, with lots of advice on drawing techniques, how to put an immense project together, keeping motivated, etc. I also like his bits on inspiration: I actually found his blog by way of a particular post that's still the best of them all, Cracking Paint and City Streets[1]. I used to love drawing maps and making castles in the mud and such when I was a kid, so this struck a chord for me.

So, on its own, there's not much to fault with the latest Dinotopia venture. It's got lovely paintings to look at, a story that gives an excuse to wander through various landscapes, and the book itself is put together beautifully. Does it add up to more than that? I was more moved by the book than I thought I would be; that's partly my inner child speaking, marvelling at the creatures and maps and funny details. But more than that, it's an odd, singular vision presented in the Dinotopia world, and I respond to worlds that are portrayed so coherently and so lovingly.

[1]http://gurneyjourney.blogspot.com/2007/10/cracking-paint-and-city-streets.html

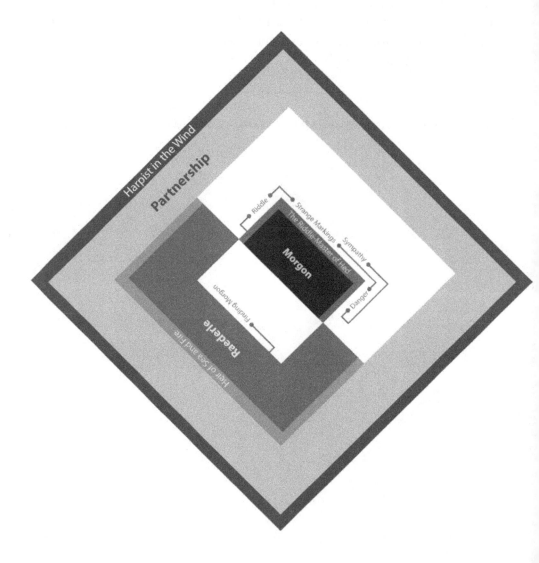

All-Star Childhood Memories

Nowadays I can pick up any pop cultural obsession that I want - hey, it's the internet age and my nerdy disposable income goes a long ways. But when I was a kid, it was almost always hard to find cool stuff.

I ended up reading a whole lot of crap, since I didn't have as much control over what I could find. In a situation like that, the formative moments are not always the ones you'd want them to be, looking back as a grown-up.

I was persistent enough, though, to find a few gems along the way, like Patricia A. McKillip's *The Riddle-Master of Hed*.

That's the first book in a trilogy, and all three books are memorable. The first book, from the year 1976, was followed by *Heir of Sea and Fire* a year later, and the saga concluded with *Harpist in the Wind* in 1979. All three are short, as far as trilogies go—all told, the trio clocks in at under 600 pages. Most epic fantasies take up that much space in a single volume!

In the first book, a young prince of Hed, Morgon, is trying to go about his life as the leader of a small island full of farmers. But he has three stars burned on his forehead, and in a world where an unanswered riddle is easily fatal, no one can answer the question posed by the strange markings.

The first book is an introduction to the world, but also a kind of abstract story. Constant danger surrounds Morgon, but it's not always clear where it's coming from or why. That puts us in sympathy with Morgon, since he's in the process of figuring out what's going on too.

The Riddle-Master of Hed is atmospheric and furnished with some imaginative magic, but a bit standard, complete with a magical young man growing up. Standard, at least until the ending! The first book concludes with a cliffhanger that frightened the heck out of me as a kid and that I still found quite chilling when I re-read it.

What's more, instead of bogging down in the second book like most fantasy trilogies do, McKillip uses the cliffhanger of the first book as an opportunity. *Heir of Sea and Fire* leaves our standard male hero dangling and picks up with a woman named Raederle. She and Morgon are destined to be together, but she's not really waiting around for her white knight. The second book is mainly about Raederle's efforts to find Morgon, and then the third book is about their partnership, which is not treated as protagonist and sidekick, but rather a duo of powerful people. Smart stuff, and it makes the trilogy tightly constructed, with two character arcs that then merge to form third. It's not entirely balanced but it's much more so than most fantasy stories.

In the introduction to the 1999 omnibus edition, McKillip talks about how Tolkien hit her like a bolt of lightning. But you would hardly know it from this book: on the scale of slavish Tolkien imitations, this one hardly registers. There might be a prophecy and a map, but all else is entirely McKillip's own marvellous work.

That's ironic praise, considering what I'm about say next: her prose and plotting have a tendency to the elliptical. Elliptical is a polite way of saying "obscure" for the books that don't work, and "intriguing" for the ones that do, like *The Riddle-Master* trilogy. These gaps are artfully done, just like everything in her novels, and they make her books very unique.

All the same, I have to confess that I haven't kept up with McKillip's recent books. Her love of the elliptical has only intensified, and I've found the plots a little too puzzling for me. If this is your fancy, that's great. In fact I'm thrilled that there's a writer out there who *isn't* churning out the same fantasy crap. In this particular case, it's a road I can't follow.

This article was the first in an informal series: revisiting the books that I read as a kid to see how they hold up. When I think of McKillip, I also think of my younger self's encounter with Robin McKinley's duo of books, The Hero and the Crown, the second book I ever bought with my own money, and The Blue Sword, the first book I ever read with a sex scene in it! See: "I Don't Remember, I Don't Recall"

I Don't Remember, I Don't Recall

Robin McKinley's *The Hero and the Crown*, a young adult fantasy novel from the early 1980s, always stood out in my memory as a formative read from childhood. Unfortunately I couldn't really say what the book was about! Over the years, everything about it had faded.

The Blue Sword, which McKinley wrote earlier but is set later in the same fantasy realm, does have a scene that I remembered: it's a sex scene, the first that I could recall reading as a kid. At least I thought it was in *The Blue Sword*...

Now that I've reread the two books, I was shocked to discover that the racy stuff actually took place in *The Hero and the Crown*!

With that kind of a mental switcheroo, it just confirms that it really was years ago that I read the books. I probably bought the *The Hero and the Crown* in grade 5 or 6, not long after I had discovered *Lord of the Rings*—yup, that's a few decades ago!

(As a digression: does anyone else remember school book fairs? I never had much money as a kid, but I did save up to buy lots of Gordon Korman books. Not many others survived from those years, but I still have Korman, McKinley, and a much-worn copy of *The Hobbit*.)

I have only one other memory of McKinley's book—and now I'm starting to doubt whether it's true. I recall looking at the cover (which depicts a giant black dragon blasting a human with fire) with some of my friends and saying, "As if this tiny person can win against this giant dragon!" If I wasn't already a smart-ass critic in grade school, at least that's what I'd like to think I was—it could very well be that my brain has filled in this anecdote...

With such a complete lack of recall, what was it like to revisit this book? That was another surprise—huge sections were instantly familiar.

While I didn't remember any specific scenes before I started reading, entire scenes, down to bits of phrasing, came back to me wholesale.

This book made a big impression on me - not in the sense that I could recall the plot points, since that was not the case. But rather that it formed so much of my reading consciousness, the way that I developed as a reader. I would go so far as to say that re-reading this book was a direct pipeline back to my childhood mind.

The Hero and the Crown is the story of Aerin, a princess who doesn't fit in with her family and wants her own purpose in life. To prove herself, she goes up against a dragon, as promised by the cover. I remember being fascinated by her attempts to create a fire-proof ointment. She confidently tests it on a bonfire; then she discovers that dragon-fire, not surprisingly, is much worse.

I haven't given away all that much about the book, since Aerin defeats the black dragon Maur by the halfway point. Much is yet to come.

The Blue Sword takes place generations later, when most magic is gone. Harry doesn't fit in with her family either, and has to prove her own worth. The writing quality is high, but it's not as polished as the later book and the story feels less smooth as well.

The Hero and the Crown won the Newberry Medal, and some of the material here made me ponder what it's like to write for a younger audience. If we can call it a responsibility, McKinley handles it with great assurance. I didn't understand everything she wrote about, back in the old days, but I never felt condescended to. In other words, this is a book that stands up to re-reading.

Growing up is not an easy thing to write about (as the lesser quality of McKinley's own *The Blue Sword* shows). Rites of passage are always about learning your own strengths, the limitations of those in authority (usually parents), and maybe a few hints of sexual maturity. Aerin becomes a sexual adult with the least of fuss—it's so matter-of-fact that the impact is magnified. Looking back, I became very curious to see if *The Hero and the Crown* would be banworthy, like perennial target Judy Blume or others, but not so. Other fantasies get banned—like chaste Harry Potter—so I'm still a little mystified. This is a happy oversight for young nerds, who wouldn't be caught dead reading Judy Blume (well, I did anyways, but it never stuck with me in the same way).

Not So Happy Ending

Talk about a long journey. Stephen King wrote the first line of a short story called "The Gunslinger" in 1970, at the beginning of his career, and the first volume of the *Dark Tower* series was published in 1982. Nearly 35 years after its humble beginnings, the series has come to its conclusion with the nearly 900 pages of the seventh volume, simply called *The Dark Tower*. Fans have been waiting for this book for a long time, and you'd think they'd trust King to wrap things up properly. Some readers like the ending, but an equally large proportion detest it.

What's the fuss?

The first and most straightforward reason is that King puts himself in the story. He first shows up as a character in the previous book— King is a writer, and many of his stories are coming true in the alternate versions of reality that the other characters come from. These characters are angry that King has given up on writing the *Dark Tower* series because that means they won't complete their quest. He's a bit of a loser and a drunk, but his writing is also the crucial difference between the end of the universe and its rejuvenation. Many bits of his other books show up in these last two *Dark Tower* books. Overall, it's a strange mix of massively swollen ego and a self-critical examination.

Including yourself in your story is a perfectly legitimate narrative strategy, but it's incredibly difficult to pull off, and it will simply never work for a large number of people (see: the typical reaction to a massively swollen ego). I don't care much for it myself, mostly because it smacks too much of a writer running out of ideas and then looking in the mirror. Metafiction like this just seems like too much of an easy temptation. A writer has to work hard to convince me otherwise, and King doesn't quite pull it off.

The second main reason for the fan hysteria is that the seventh book seems to be written by a different person. Simply put, King has undergone huge changes in his thinking about the series. The easiest way to explain it is by analogy. Michael Whelan, noted sf illustrator, provided the cover and interior illustrations for the very first *Dark Tower* book and now the very last one. It's no accident that the main character of the *Dark Tower,* Roland, looks a lot like Clint Eastwood in Whelan's illustrations (especially in this book)—the hero was clearly drawn from Eastwood's persona when King first started writing. That was back in the early 1970s, when Eastwood had made his mark in spaghetti westerns and was moving into the era of *Dirty Harry* and even more violent revenge fantasies.

While the comparison is not a strictly accurate one (and I don't want to give away much about the ending), King's version of the hero six books later is like what Eastwood did with his own persona in the revisionist *Unforgiven. Unforgiven* ruthlessly cuts down everything about the way that most such stories use an ultaviolent antihero, essentially a psychotic killer, as an engine of the story. In one sense, Eastwood was punishing Dirty Harry. The problem for King is that *Unforgiven* is a different movie than *The Good, the Bad, and the Ugly* or *Dirty Harry*. People who hate *Unforgiven* can go back to enjoying the days when Clint looked down the barrel of his gun and said, "Are you feeling lucky, punk?" King has put this revised hero in the same series. If you like the driven, amoral Roland of the first few *Dark Tower* books, you might not be happy with what happens to him later.

While I applaud this change, and I appreciated the ending of the series, consider this: you're reading an epic fantasy, you've been looking forward to the ending for (perhaps literally) your whole life as a reader, you love the characters, you hiss at the villains, and so forth. Can you demand a happy ending? What are your rights as a reader? I have no answer to these questions, but I can understand the point of someone who has gotten deeply into the story and feels let down by the ending.

Ironically, King's slow pace at completing the series likely made things worse for his most compulsive readers. I think that someone who picks up the first book and reads all seven in a row, now that all are available, might be mystified by the big fuss. If you've been building expectations in your head for twenty years, any conclusion could be a let-down.

The Trouble with Endings

I've noticed recently that otherwise good stories have been let down by their endings. It's partly due to the expectations of the audience: you can imagine any kind of ending you want, but when the ending finally arrives, it's been narrowed down to a single one of those possibilities and it might not be as good as the one in your head. I argued this was the case for Stephen King's *Dark Tower* series.

The other reason for a bad ending: nobody in charge thought about it. And in the case of *Minority Report*, the filmmakers clearly had *no freaking idea* what to do with the conclusion of the story, and decided to just keep throwing more and more junk at the screen.

I was thinking about *Minority Report* and its painful ending because I recently watched the zombie movie *28 Days Later*. As far as zombie flicks go, it was reasonably creepy, at least until I started watching some of the extras on the DVD. Not only was there an alternate ending, there was an alternate last half. The creative team had a solid premise, but the ending, such as it was, suddenly felt very arbitrary to me.

It's certainly true that when a writer of any kind is looking at a story, they'll consider a number of different conclusions. That's normal, but the process is best served by picking one that fits the tone and (for lack of a better word) meaning of the story. If you don't know how to end your movie or book, to me that's a sign that you don't know what your story is about or how it will affect the audience.

Now, what movie did this remind me of? Oh yeah, *Minority Report*.

I actually give fairly high marks to this movie. It has a strong pedigree: it's based on a short story by Philip K. Dick, one of the notable writers in the genre (and whose novel *Do Androids Dream of Electric Sheep?* was filmed as *Blade Runner*); it's directed by Steven Spielberg, who is no slouch in the blockbuster scifi department; and it stars Tom Cruise, who despite being a bland-y superstar has actually acted for some of the best directors (Stanley Kubrick and Ridley Scott among them).

Minority Report also has a high dose of the cognitive kick that makes for the best science fiction. The movie takes Dick's idea—policing based on precognition—and collides it full tilt into recent notions of the surveillance society. It's wildly scary when advertisers know your every purchasing habit, the police have a way of predicting what you'll do and arrest you before you've committed a crime, and there's no escape from this dazzling matrix of social control.

I should also mention that the movie has some awesome action sequences. The best two are a pair that happen right in the middle of the movie. Tom Cruise is on the run, and he is up against a squad of cops who have jetpacks (a scene that keenly demonstrates the movie's sardonic sense of humour). He also fights the police in a fully-automated car factory—lots o' destruction.

Now, it's a bit absurd to show a future that has *completely* destroyed the freedom of the individual, then fall back on nonsensical action movie heroics as the way out. That's not a surprise, seeing how the plot of most Hollywood scifi movies are constructed, but it's still absurd in this context.

The bigger sin of the movie is easy to summarize: the ending stinks. For several reasons. The first is that the plot holes begin to accumulate, and if you're the kind of person who cares about that kind of stuff, it gets on your nerves. Why is the police building so poorly secured? The people with precognition—they can apparently only see murders ahead of time, but later on a chase sequence directly contradicts this. And so forth.

I'm more worried about two other aspects of the ending. People call it a false ending when you think the story is over but it keeps going. At the cheapest level, this is like the slasher movie villain who doesn't die. *Minority Report* is a little more sophisticated but it still has about half an hour of screen time at the conclusion that takes place after the apparent finale. I understand that this is a valid narrative trick, but it has to be done well or your audience will be annoyed with you. You have to earn it with something striking as a payoff.

That's related to my other point about the ending. Writing a story about a totalitarian society is tricky because the denouement for any individual is almost always tragic. If you want a happy ending, you have to work hard to convince the audience either: a) the protagonist brought down the system single-handedly; or b) the protagonist happened to live at the historical moment when a great number of people brought about change together. *Minority Report* wants option a) for Tom Cruise, along with a romantic ending, and it doesn't feel right in comparison to all the hard work the movie did earlier convincing us of the scary and terrible nature of this societal system.

The Cultural Gutter

Explaining Vampires

Butler's death in February 2006 was a huge loss. This article would have been much different in the post-Twilight era.

I don't care that much for vampire stories. It's a reflexive dislike that's hard to define—basically, I'm not part of the target audience of the whole vampire fascination.

Another pet peeve of mine is the amnesiac protagonist. What an absolutely lame excuse to explain everything to the audience! When I see that a book features memory loss, I put it down with scarcely another glance.

So it's a good thing that I ignored my prejudices and read Octavia E. Butler's *Fledgling*, a story of a young vampire girl named Shori who wakes up in the forest with no memory of her previous life or how she got there.

An amnesiac vampire... how does Butler pull it off? For one thing, *Fledgling* shows Butler at the top of her writing game, which takes away some of the pain of the amnesia storyline. In terms of vampire stereotypes, Butler succumbs to none of them: Shori's story is the furthest thing from an Anne Rice ripoff imaginable.

The quality of Butler's writing is astonishing—the book is strong, clear, and grabs you even if you don't want to go along (which was my case). I would rate her work easily the equal of Ursula K. Le Guin; like Le Guin's recent YA fantasy *Gifts*, the prose here is never too ornate but it also retains an undeniable esthetic power. It feels right, and it feels compelling.

Vampire stories almost inevitably deal in themes of power and sexuality. What would it be like to be under the thrall of a ruthless being like Dracula? Ooo, scary. Butler flips all that on its head by telling the story from Shori's point of view. And Shori is an intensely sympathetic character, starting with the first thing that we know about her—her entire family has been murdered and then burned to ash along with everything else in their village. Butler keeps these opening segments of the book popping along, and before we know it, we're firmly on Shori's side.

It's true that Shori sucks blood, and this act binds a human irretrievably to her will if it happens more than two or three times. But Butler keeps our sympathy by making Shori a member of a vampire faction that respects humans and is fighting against a splinter group that's much worse. The ideas and themes of the book are subversive because we can't help but identify with Shori, the enemy. It's empathy whether we want it or not.

Butler was not alone in choosing to write a vampire novel after making a reputation with other types of fiction. The biggest other example is Robin McKinley, the well-known YA fantasy author, who wrote a book called *Sunshine* a few years ago. I decided to read *Sunshine* after running across a comment by Suzy McKee Charnas: as someone who also writes vampire stories, she was making an insider's complaint that *Sunshine* explains things in blinding detail. Feeling bold, I would widen the complaint to say that this happens to vampire novels in general, especially if you include Elizabeth Kostova's bestselling *The Historian*.

I suppose it's a matter of life and death, as illustrated by *Fledgling*. Shori will die if she doesn't figure out the intricacies of vampire life and vulnerability. In most other books, it's the humans who need to figure out if garlic works, if a wooden stake will kill, and so forth.

Another thing struck me, less while reading *Fledgling* and more with regard to *The Historian*. A topic like vampires is so widely written about that the topic attracts a lot of minutia—is this a vampire like a Stephen King *or* an Anne Rice vampire? Or like a Buffy vampire? The differences are crucial to those involved in the fictional perils (ironically, this is something that I've noticed all fictional characters in a vampire story talk about!). In a vicious circle, a writer like Kostova then has to write 600 pages of hardcore history to differentiate her take on vampires from the umpteen other ones.

On a slightly different topic, what does it mean that all of the writers mentioned here (with the exception of Stephen King) have been women? I'm really not sure, since vampire fiction itself varies so much. I would put Butler and McKinley and Kostova in a higher bracket of quality than writers who specialize in vampire fiction like

Anne Rice or Laurell K. Hamilton, but this is my own bias showing. All the same, female dominance in writing vampire fiction of all kinds would take a whole new article to unravel.

A sad note to end with. Octavia E. Butler died just a few months ago, and *Fledgling* was her last book. Butler was a unique figure, a writer who brought enormous quality to the science fiction that she wrote. I highly recommend all of her books; *Fledgling* is a good place to start, even if it does stand apart from her other books.

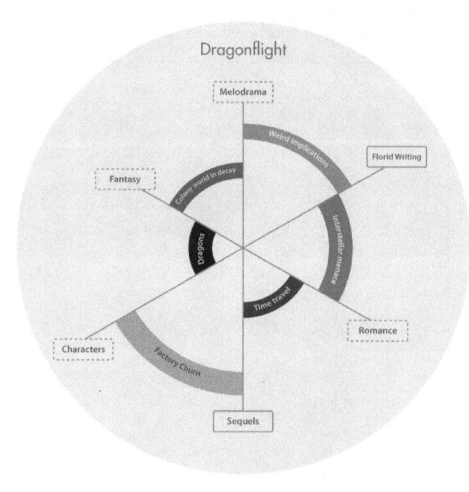

So Awesome, Then Churned Out by a Factory

This has been the biggie: I've started re-reading the Pern series by Anne McCaffrey. Wow, talk about a trip! I had almost completely forgotten the series and its impact on me years ago. I think this was due to the excessive sequels that tarnished the creativity of the project.

But now that I've re-read *Dragonflight*, the book that started the whole Pern deal way back in 1968, I feel like I've discovered a lost chunk of my brain. The first book is completely crazed—it's got dozens of science fiction ideas thrown into a wild mix of melodrama, and it explodes in six different directions at once.

Here is a quick list of the main concepts that McCaffrey jams into one 250-page book:

- Dragons—they fly, they teleport, they belch flame

- Time travel—I won't add any other spoilers, but McCaffrey gets pretty heavily into paradoxes and timelines

- Colony world in decay—Pern is a planet that was colonized by an advanced society long ago but that has now fallen into primitive times (this one has been used hundreds of times in science fiction but seldom so effectively)

- Interstellar menace—spores from outer space, the "Red Star" to be more specific, fall as "Threads" from the sky for fifty years, followed by a two hundred year gap—a "Thread" will kill all organic life that it touches

- Weird implications of all of the above—McCaffrey is quite adept at figuring out the social consequences of all these things and creating an interesting story, which is very difficult!

It's this last point which probably makes the whole book so vivid. For example, the colonists genetically engineered dragons to burn Threads from the sky, but the gaps between the passes of the Red Star are long enough that ordinary people resent supporting the dragonmen. In *Dragonflight*, these kinds of details are worked out with extraordinary flair.

McCaffrey also throws in a ton of melodrama, and I see this as a large part of the appeal of visiting Pern. There's always some kind of personal conflict going on—I think McCaffrey's cast of characters was my introduction to people *who just don't get along*. The first book also adapted a large part of its plot structure from romance: strongwilled young girl, authoritative older man ... throw them together with some peril and watch the fireworks.

Best of all, the dragons and time travel and interstellar spores are just background for the tumultuous lives of people we soon care about or dislike intensely. I'm not saying that the wacky SF ideas are superfluous—more that we learn about them as part of the trials and tribulations of interesting characters.

Dragonflight displays quite a florid writing style on McCaffrey's part. It's a bit hard to pin down precisely, but I think it might be in the use of adverbs. Everyone is either "lounging indolently" or "drawling sardonically" or some such thing. McCaffrey doesn't seem able to turn down any rhetorical trick that would amp up the immediate impact of the story.

I loved the Pern books, but I kind of lost interest in the series as the "churned out by a factory" quotient went up and not much new was going on. Sequels are always dicey propositions to me. I like "more of the same" just like everyone else, but it gets boring after a while. If a book is just coasting on its predecessors, it gets obvious fast. Prequels are much worse, since there's often no hope of anything new at all. In that sense, I'm a novelty junkie—I actually don't want to know how the Pernese dragons were developed, or how the Threads first hit Pern. That stuff is great as backstory. Front and centre, it's just a drag.

But now that I've re-read *Dragonflight*, I can see where the various sequels and prequels came from—they're all in this book already. The second book, *Dragonquest*, deals with tensions with a group called the "oldtimers" and they first arrive on the scene here, while the third book, *The White Dragon*, has a protagonist who had a very dramatic birth in this book. Durable characters—like Robinton the masterharper—were here, and a whole framework of craftholder life sets up the *Dragondrums* trilogy. The legend of Moreta, queen dragon-rider of the ancient past, is mentioned with reverence, and sure enough, she gets her own book later too.

That's about where I lost interest in the series—quite a few books followed. I take the point that McCaffrey is painting on a broad canvas of thousands of years, but after a such a mind-numbing quantity of sequels, everything compelling and unique has long been done. I knew that part, but I was glad to be reminded of the superb quality of *Dragonflight*. Turns out that I wasn't crazy to be enthused about the series in the first place!

Smooth, Smoother, Smoothest

When I read the second and third Attolia books later, I was happy to discover that they are just as good as the first book.

I get sucked in very easily by books that are smooth on the surface. If a book has glossy enough writing and a well-paced storyline, then I'm almost always a sucker for it. But when a book also has something intriguing going on underneath the surface, then I feel like my optimism has been rewarded—and that's when I really love a book. Enter Megan Whalen Turner's *The Thief*.

The Thief is a young adult novel from about a decade ago. It was Turner's first novel, and kicked up some fuss, including a Newberry Honor. It's ostensibly labelled fantasy, and you can easily read it that way. But it's closer to Guy Gavriel Kay's way of creating historical alternates than, say, *Dungeons & Dragons*. In this case, Turner models ancient Greek city-states, with a few anachronisms like guns, and a very subtle case of polytheism. That the gods are listening makes it a fantasy? I guess. There's also a quest for a magic object.

Gen is in the king's prison; he's the thief of the title. The king's advisor, the magus, will free Gen on one condition: that Gen helps him steal the aforementioned magic object. The magic doodad, Hamiathes's Gift, will apparently guarantee the holder the kingship of a neighbouring country. The magus, Gen, and a few soldiers go on a trek, locate the hiding spot, then turn the success of the expedition over to Gen and his thieving ways. All along, they've been telling each other stories of their gods and goddesses.

The bits and pieces in my summary resemble a stereotypical fantasy novel much more so than when you're reading the book. The difference is in the characterization I guess, since there are some remarkable moments along the way, and some puzzling aspects click together with resounding elegance at the end. It's adventure, sure, but unexpectedly coherent and impressive.

The difference is also in the smooth writing. Turner's style reminds me a great deal of Ursula K. Le Guin, who always stands in for smooth prose when I think about such things. *The Thief* is like a less gloomy version of Le Guin's *The Tombs of Atuan*, to be perhaps too precise.

Turner has written two sequels. I must say, though, that as much as I'm looking forward to those next two books, *The Queen of Attolia* and *The King of Attolia*, the delicious sense of anticipation—yes, the author has written some more books in the series!—is mingled with a large proportion of wariness. I'm jaded, but I've been burned too many times. It's started to affect my enjoyment of a book, even if it stands alone.

A few examples to illustrate. My clearest example is always *His Dark Materials* by Philip Pullman. I loved *The Golden Compass*, thought *The Subtle Knife* (book two) was ok, and hated the concluding book, *The Amber Spyglass*. But even if the follow-up books are not giant disappointments, they very seldom live up to the first book. I liked Garth Nix's *Sabriel* quite a lot, but books two and three were simply... passable. Similarly, one of the reader reviews for *The Thief* on Amazon mentioned a similarity to Lian Hearn's *Tales of the Otori*, which brought back a flood of memories for me. I had managed to block that series from my mind for years, so I went back and checked my notes. Sure enough, I loved the first book, but as it turns out, books two and three were awesome too - right up until the grand finale, which was hideous and random. I had been burned by recommending *The Golden Compass* to a bunch of people before finishing the series myself, so I was holding off on doing the same for Hearn's series. It looked so promising! And book three so good too, I was looking for boxed sets for gifts, the whole deal.

Will the same thing happen for Turner? I'm a weird mix of gloom and optimism, as I've mentioned: I would love to have an example to counter my reasons for despair. At this point, all I can say for sure is that I'm glad that *The Thief* is a relatively self-contained work, just like *Sabriel* by Nix. If the next two books are ho-hum, I'll just have to come back and read the first one again.

The Nature of the Hero, Rowling-Style

A few months ago, I decided to take the plunge: I would burn through the Harry Potter series, now complete, all in one go. It's been... interesting. I've discovered all kinds of things I had not realized before, including the fact that Harry is—to put it diplomatically—not a particularly effective hero.

When I decided to plow through the series, I had what turned out to be a fair number of misconceptions. In each book, he fights Voldemort at the end, and there's a bunch of "British boarding school" material that fills in the rest of it. Not so! The boarding school stuff is omnipresent, but it all supports two themes:

- The nature of the hero, specifically Harry

- Growing up

None of this is groundbreaking stuff, per se, but Rowling handles it extraordinarily well. In terms of growing up, books 5 and 6 have a lot more material about romance, and how relationships are not a particularly easy thing when you're a teenager. Some of this feels about as painful as reality (fortunately not at the *Freaks and Geeks* level of gritty painfulness—I've been catching up on my iconic-yet-cancelled TV shows). In general, Harry is learning more about the adult world (in this case, the wizarding world) each year, and he gets more and more entangled in adult things like racism and dishonesty, and the rather grim realization that mistakes you made in your life years ago can cause problems much further down the road.

As for the nature of Harry the hero, I made a claim that he's ineffective, but this is not necessarily a bad thing. For one thing, he gets a lot of hype around him, but his lack of perfection humanizes him in a way that a more heroic version might not. As Rowling has portrayed him, Harry is a convincing mix of hot-headed and naive; in the later books, he gets quite angry. If he was always calm and perfectly in control and all-powerful, he would be another Dumbledore! (Considerations of Dumbledore's character would be an entirely different column).

I would draw a parallel between Harry and Buffy, another "heroic" character, another "Chosen One" (both series use this exact phrase, making my comparison a little too easy), and while both would much rather have a normal life, they don't lay down their burdens. I would say that Harry is a much angrier character than Buffy, who had her roots in her "Valley Girl goes into a dark alley and comes out triumphant" high-concept. Harry comes out of a Roald Dahl tradition, whose influences I would argue are particularly strong on the first book. As he grows up, he becomes much more susceptible to rage - against the Dahl-esque Dursleys, against all the circumstances arrayed against him. He knows that he should control his anger, but how can he? It's a horrible burden.

Harry gets by with generous help from other people. An idealized loner hero? Not here. The series is essentially the process by which Harry accumulates the friends and surrogate family to help him defeat evil (which makes another parallel to Buffy's story). Harry on his own is not an effective hero, but because of his friendly nature, he has drawn people to him.

Some of this is explained rather explicitly in books five and six once Dumbledore tells Harry a bit about the nature of the prophecy that pits Voldemort against Harry specifically. Not to give too much away, but it boils down to this: Harry's not so much a hero as an outward manifestation of Voldemort's innate characters flaws that will eventually bring the Dark Lord down. Voldemort wanted to strike, and in striking, created his worst enemy. Harry's actions function in the opposite way: he draws people to him, turning them to the good side for their own reasons, not fear.

I mentioned another major misconception on my part. I've learned that Harry hardly ever fights Voldemort! I don't want to give away every ending in the series, so I'll just say that Rowling provides a number of other interesting twists and turns.

As for the finish of the series, I thought that the build-up to the ending was terrific, really exciting stuff, but the ending itself was fairly... technical. Harry made an assumption based on arcane mechanics of a certain kind of magic, which required a lot of explanation. Maybe not that different than the info-dumps required at the end of the previous

Potter books? And secondly, I'm dismayed that the movie-makers have chosen to split the the seventh book into two movies, since book 7 is probably the best candidate for compression. If Movie 7 Part 1 is all the camping bits from the first half of The Deathly Hallows, I'll happily skip that one.

My favourite book is definitely number six, Harry Potter and the Half-Blood Prince. It's a compelling mix of the humourous moments from the start of the series with the more grown-up material from later on. As for Harry himself, he has yet to prove himself to others, but he feels like much more of his own person. And it's less bloated than the previous book, Harry Potter and the Order of the Phoenix.

The Cultural Gutter

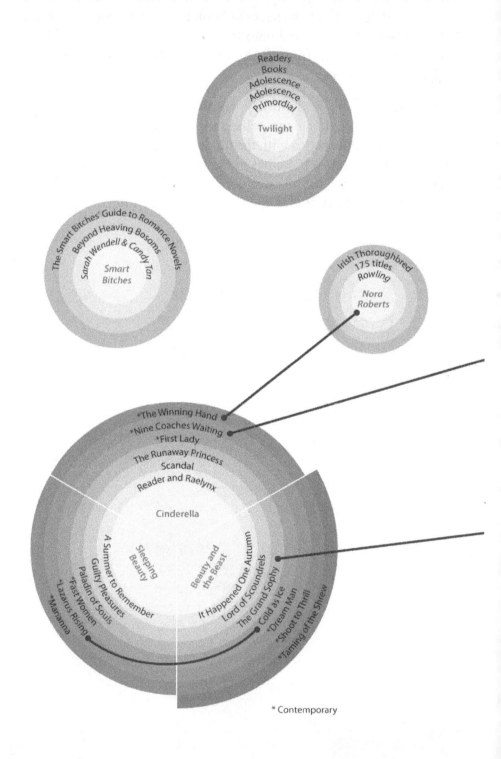

Readers
Books
Adolescence
Adolescence
Primordial

Twilight

The Smart Bitches' Guide to Romance Novels
Beyond Heaving Bosoms
Sarah Wendell & Candy Tan

Smart
Bitches

Irish Thoroughbred
175 titles
Rowling

Nora
Roberts

*The Winning Hand
*Nine Coaches Waiting
*First Lady
The Runaway Princess
Scandal
Reader and Raelynx

Cinderella

A Summer to Remember
Guilty Pleasures
Paladin of Souls
*Fast Women
*Lazarus Rising
*Marianna

Sleeping
Beauty

Beauty and
the Beast

It Happened One Autumn
Lord of Scoundrels
The Grand Sophy
Cold as Ice
*Dream Man
*Shoot to Thrill
*Taming of the Shrew

* Contemporary

ROMANCE

Chris Szego

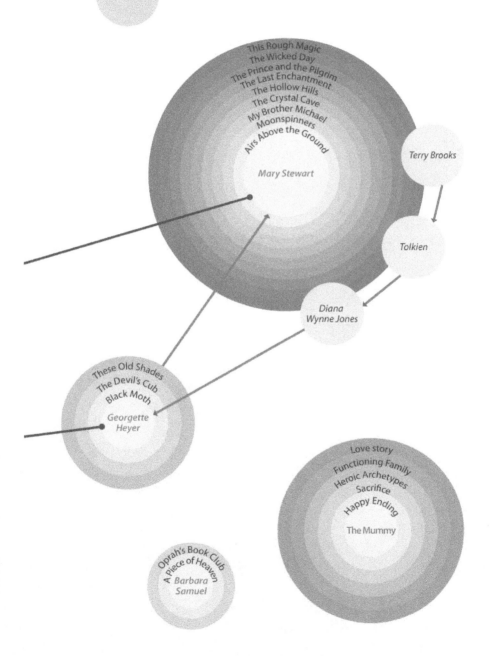

R.W.A.

This Rough Magic
The Wicked Day
The Prince and the Pilgrim
The Last Enchantment
The Hollow Hills
The Crystal Cave
My Brother Michael
Moonspinners
Airs Above the Ground

Mary Stewart

Terry Brooks

Tolkien

Diana
Wynne Jones

These Old Shades
The Devil's Cub
Black Moth

Georgette
Heyer

Love story
Functioning Family
Heroic Archetypes
Sacrifice
Happy Ending

The Mummy

Oprah's Book Club
A Piece of Heaven
Barbara
Samuel

Love For Sale

It is an untruth universally acknowledged that a woman in possession of a romance novel must be in want of A) wits, B) a social life, or C) both.

I read romance, and frankly don't care what other people think that says about me. In fact, I think the bias itself says some pretty interesting things. There's a lot to unpack in the pervasive and persistent stereotype that surrounds the romance section of any given bookstore. I see that stereotype emerging from three directions: lack of knowledge of the genre and its readers; envy; and the belief that romances are badly written. But it could be argued that it stems from one source.

First, some background. A study released by the ABA in 2002[1] exploded a number of myths about romance readers. For one thing, they were well-educated. Compared to the national average, romance readers were vastly more likely to have finished some form of post-secondary study. They also expressed a substantially higher than average sense of of job satisfaction. Possibly as a corollary, they also indicated comfort with their earning power. And—this one was a bit of a surprise—they had solid romantic relationships. Something like eighty percent self-identified as happy in their marriages/long-term partnerships. So much for the bored and lonely housewife desperately seeking something to fill her empty days.

There are other more accessible, and more startling, statistics that pertain to romance novels: sales numbers. Romance readers buy more books, more often, than any other group. That certainly shows up on the bottom line—across all formats, romance novels account for more than 35% of fiction sales. When considering only mass-market paperbacks, the number jumps to 54% of *books*. To put it another way, when it comes to paperbacks, *romances sell more than all other genres and subjects combined*. Such obvious success makes romance an easy target; there's no point in scorning something off the radar. Sales of that magnitude mean that midlist romance novelists can make a living, unsupported by arts council grants, even. That kind of thing always draws envy of the bitterest kind.

As for being badly written... well, yeah, sometimes that's true. Some romances are poorly written indeed. So are some mysteries, some biographies, many business books, and most undergraduate poetry. Theodore Sturgeon said that ninety percent of everything is crap—romance is no exception. Why should it be?

The lack of awareness, the jealousy, the scorn: these are only symptoms of a deeper disease. Truth is, romances are primarily written by, and for, women. Even today, that automatically relegates them to second-tier status. Detractors claim that romance novels foster unrealistic expectations in readers that can interfere in real-life relationships. Er, pardon? Most of the western world read Harry Potter, and did anyone claim it made readers believe magic was real? (Okay, the lunatic fringe tried, but they could find witchcraft in breakfast cereal, and were rightfully ignored by the wider world) But apparently romance readers—who are, don't forget, well-educated and by-and-large happily involved—can't tell fiction from reality. It's the same old story: women can't be trusted to know what they want.

Bugger that.

As a bookseller, I respect the enormous sales of romance novels. They've kept many a publisher in the black. As a reader, I simply enjoy them. Good stories, well told are always a pleasure. And I'm not alone in my appreciation. Let's face it: if you recognized the mangled quote that opened this essay, you've read a romance, too.

---

1 These statistics were taken from a study conducted by the RWA and the ABA in 2002. The RWA updates this study periodically. To see their most recent results, see their website at: http://www.rwanational.org/cs/the_romance_genre/romance_literature_statistics

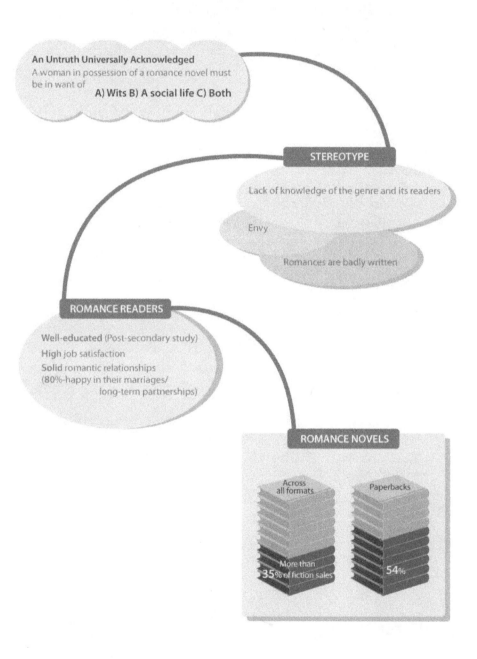

An Untruth Universally Acknowledged
A woman in possession of a romance novel must be in want of
A) Wits B) A social life C) Both

STEREOTYPE

Lack of knowledge of the genre and its readers

Envy

Romances are badly written

ROMANCE READERS

Well-educated (Post-secondary study)
High job satisfaction
Solid romantic relationships
(80%-happy in their marriages/
long-term partnerships)

ROMANCE NOVELS

Across all formats
More than 35% of fiction sales

Paperbacks
54%

It's Fun to go the R.W.A.

The internet allows writers to do the impossible: write in isolation while in company. A writer might still face off single-handedly against blank screen, but behind the accusing blink of the cursor there are thousands of minds ready to offer information, support and catwaxing options. On the other hand, it's not as if, pre-internet, every writer was locked in a Proustian cork-lined room. Despite the solitary nature of their work—or possibly because of it—writers have always sought one another out. For encouragment, professional development, and sometimes for the sheer relief of being around other people who get it. That's pretty much the unofficial definition of the RWA.

Romantic fiction became popular during the Regency era, when writers like Jane Austen were read by absolutely everyone. The genre slowly began to coalesce through the nineteenth and twentieth centuries, but in the 1970s, it kicked into high gear. At the end of that decade, several women decided to form a group to pool their knowledge and experience, and to help one another with both the creative and business aspects of writing romance. There were thirty-seven members when the Romance Writers of America was formed in 1980. Today, there are more than ten thousand from all around the world.

The RWA is a major non-profit trade organization, with ten staff, an elected Board of Directors, dedicated committee volunteers, and many mind-numbing pages of bylaws. Its mission statement is: "to advance the professional interests of career-focused romance writers through networking and advocacy". And damn, do they follow through.

Joining the RWA gives a writer access to an amazing amount of information about the genre, about writing, and about the publishing industry as a whole. The Romance Writer's Report, the member magazine, contains interviews, writing tips, market information, sales numbers, and much more. But that's just the beginning. Once a writer joins the national organization, she can also join any of its 145 chapters. Some of the chapters have to do with subject matter, like the Kiss of Death chapter, which focuses on romantic suspense. Others, like the Toronto Romance Writers, are strictly based on location. But the highlight of the year is the annual national conference.

Known simply as "National", the massive conference brings editors, agents, reviewers, artists, and marketers together with thousands of writers, then hits 'blend'. There are workshops, pitch sessions, lectures, spotlight hours, and more parties than the Toronto International Film Festival. Sales are made at the conference, deals struck and careers born. It's an exhilarating, exhausting rush.

The RWA is no slouch when it comes to advocacy, either. Its members know how the genre is perceived in popular culture: they also know what it's worth (in 2008, for instance, it was worth $1.37 *billion* in sales alone). They attend Book Expo and other major trade shows, operate a Speaker's Bureau, provide libraries and booksellers with lists and catalogues, and compile statistics for common use. Several years ago they created a continent-wide poster campaign, similar in function (though not style) to the 'look who's in our library' campaign of the '90s. They maintain a solid website[1] at which, among other duties, acts as a platform site for member websites, and provides a monthly list of member-written new releases. They admister awards to industry professionals, and even provide an academic grant to foster the serious study of the romance genre as a whole.

The RWA is also dedicated to furthering literacy. Which may sound self-serving, but they've accomplished a great deal at both the community and federal levels. Since 1991, the RWA has raised over $600K for literacy programs. The main fund-raiser is the big Literacy Autographing session which kicks off National each year. Open to the public in addition as well as attendees, it's like a candy store for the literate. Mmm, just picture it: hundreds of writers lining row upon row of long tables heaped with books (the lineup for Nora Roberts usually circles the auditorium). Publishers donate the books, and all proceeds go to literacy.

Then there are the RITA awards. They're kind of like the OSCARs of the romance world, except there are more rounds of judging. There's a similar contest for unpublished manuscripts, called the Golden Heart. Finalists in that contest end up with their work in front of major editors. It's terrific exposure, and many a Golden Heart winner ceases to be unpublished shortly thereafter.

Of course, no group is without blemish, and the RWA is no exception. Several years ago a surprisingly bigoted Board had a referendum to see whether a romance should be defined as the love story between "the two main characters" or "a man and a woman". After voting for the former, I cancelled my membership, not wanting to belong to a group that even considered the latter acceptable. I was far from alone in that action ("two main characters" passed, by the way).

Another point of contention is that alone amoung professional writers' groups, the RWA does not require publishing credits to join. However to join PAN, the Published Author's Network within the RWA, with its separate newsgroup, own information stream, and private conference track, one certainly has to produce those credits. And those credits mean something. When Harlequin announced it was going to start steering rejected manuscripts towards its newly formed vanity press, the RWA immediately removed Harlequin from its list of approved publishers. In other words, the world's largest publisher of romance was no longer be deemed an acceptable credit for PAN membership, nor could it use RWA resources at National or elsewhere. David spanked Goliath public, and other writers groups followed suit.

It has its faults—everyone does—but the RWA is truly an extraordinary organization. It is a powerhouse, large enough to be a voice the publishing industry listens to. But true to the nature of its thirty-seven founders, it is also welcoming and co-operative, and provides countless opportunties for personal growth and connection.

1 http://www.rwanational.org

She's the One

Like authors in every genre, romance writers cover a broad spectrum of imaginative ground. They come from a variety of backgrounds, and write to any number of inner aesthetics. Each one has a preferred archetype. From the bewilderingly naive traditional, to the often bloody thriller, and every permutation inbetween, romance authors write to their personal tastes in terms of pace, mood, and degree of modernity. But if you were to get a group of romance writers together and ask them about their formative influences, the vast majority will mention one name: Georgette Heyer.

Born in Wimbleton in 1903, Georgette Heyer was very much a woman of her time, which is to say cultered, educated, and above all, discreet. She was a success with her very first book, *Black Moth*, published when she was nineteen, and remained so for the rest of her life. In fact, when her husband decided to change careers, from mining engineer to barrister, it was her writing which supported the family: this, in the post WWI era, made her even more unique. When she died in 1974, she had more than fifty books in print, all of the bestsellers. But she never gave a single interview, nor did she ever make a single public appearance. No booksignings, no launches: nothing. After she married at twenty-three, she lived her private life as Mrs. Ronald Rougier. And though she said that anything anyone needed to know about her could be discovered in her books, she had four of her early novels suppressed because she felt they were too autobiographical.

Black Moth is a story full of Georgian highwaymen and derring-do that she originally created to entertain her convalescent brother. Later, Heyer redeveloped some of the characters and featured them in *These Old Shades*, a marvellous court comedy set largely in pre-Revolution Paris. Later still, the son of the two main characters in *These Old Shades* got his own book, *The Devil's Cub*. So in many ways, she was the precursor of that standard of today's publishing indurstry, the spinoff novel. But that's not why Heyer is universally adored. What makes her such a seminal figure in the development of the modern romance was her ability to immerse readers in time and place, and the indefinable something called 'voice'.

Most, though not all, of Heyer's novels are set in the British Regency. In the strict sense, the British Regency spanned the years between 1811 and 1820, when King George III was declared insane and his eldest son, the Prince of Wales, was made Prince Regent (though the broader Regency period is often extended to mean 1800-1830). Heyer's novels are sparklig clear windows into that time. Historical accuracy was vital to her, and her research into fashions, mores, and locations was intense. She lived in the cities she wrote about most often: Bath, London, York—and she investigated each from every possible aspect. Clothing, conveyances, street cant: every detail is spot on. In fact, one of her historicals novels set around the battle of Waterloo was used in history classes for many years. Her ability to catapult readers deep into other times is one of her great gifts.

The other, her inimitable voice, is harder to quantify. Certainly it has to do with her ability to create characters worth caring about, people with real feelings and real motiviations. It's also apparent in her brilliant dialogue. Often imitated by her successors though never quite duplicated, Heyer created a standard for witty banter that has rarely been equalled, and she did it consistently. But above all, her work is infused with charm. Not the facile sort that is easily forgotten, but the real thing: an allure that fascinates and delights, to a level that could almost be considered magic.

For those who just can't quite bring themselves to try one of her romances, Heyer also wrote a dozen mystery novels. They too are historically accurate, though in their case the time period was Heyer's own. Set in what was to Heyer the modern day, her mysteries have the tightly woven feel of detective novels written before the age of DNA evidence, when character-reading and clue-following reigned supreme. Her husband, a QC, vetted her plots for accuracy. Reading them now offers a remarkable glimpse into English life between and following two World Wars, and the changing nature of societal interactions.

Whether writing hard-bitten mystery, piercingly accurate history or frothy romance, Georgette Heyer occupies a plane of her own. In particular, when it comes to romance, she was a trail-blazer. Hundred of writers have followed in her footsteps. And if none have quite measured up, they have still managed to create a particularly strong and popular subgenre in her honour, called simply 'Regency'.

All That Fairy Tale Nonsense

One of the many criticisms levelled at romance novels is that they're a poor model for women when it comes to real-life relationships. All that fairy tale nonsense, detractors say, will make women want the wrong things from their partners. I could list a dozen things wrong with that assumption, but I'll limit myself to three.

First, the blanket belief that alone among the literate romance readers believe everything they read is seriously insulting. Second, it demonstrates that said detractors don't read much modern romance, or they'd know the kind of realism one can find therein. That's annoying. Is divorce realistic, or abuse, or loss? Don't worry: they're covered. (Also, please consider what that means about the nature of 'realism'). Third: fairy tales, yes, but nonsense? Please. Bruno Bettleheim would open a can of Jungian whoopass on such ignorance, and rightfully so.

Fairy tales are a subset of folk tales, and folktales are the backbone of literature. They are *powerful*. These are the stories that outlive nations. Religions may try to bury them, and political regimes to repress them, but folktalkes just don new clothes, get new haircuts, and keep going. As a kid I read hundreds, devouring one textbook-sized collection of international stories after another. So by the time I hit junior high I'd recognized that the same patterns appeared in stories from every part of the globe. This story might have a fairy godmother where that one had a talking fox; this beast might be a lion where that one was a snake. But the basic patterns, the archtypes, were the same, whether the story came from France or Russia, from India or China. That's not nonsense, it's nuclear.

So, yes, romance novels often play off patterns found in fairy and folk tales. Which is another way of saying they're tied into the beating heart of the narrative impulse. They're the stories that chronicle women's lives and their hopes, which are at least as realistic as their miseries. Fairy tales can encompass just about any setting, problem or character. In some ways, they're the ultimate in fan fiction: since the pattern is already established, writers need only to allude to it to establish emotional resonance. I can't list all the archtypes here, so for the sake of symmetry, here are the three I think are most common in modern romances.

Beauty and the Beast This is one of my personal favourites. From Persephone onward, in this story the underlying archetype is that sacrifice is rewarded... and that men are capable of change. Though the beastly character isn't always the hero: *Taming of the Shrew* is a Beauty and Beast story too. Of course nowadays beastliness isn't a matter of looks but of behavior. So the beast in question might go from withdrawn to engaged; from rapaciously ambitious to sharing; or from reckless hedonism to committed monogamy. Don't be fooled, it's not an easy trip for anyone involved. But it's worth it.

If you like historical romance try: *Lord of Scoundrels* by Loretta Chase; *The Grand Sophy* by Georgette Heyer; *It Happened One Autumn* by Lisa Kleypas.

If you prefer contemporary: *Shoot to Thrill* by Nina Bruhns; *Dream Man* by Linda Howard; *Cold as Ice* by Anne Stuart.

Cinderella The hardworking heroine of any of this wide group of stories epitomizes successful transformation. But the trappings are the least important part of her elevation. It's not about the slipper, it's about the change in state. There might be a literal move from rags to riches, but more often Cinderella stories feature characters who move from emotional paucity to abundance. Not surprisingly, this is one of the most popular archetypes. After all, if there's one thing women know how to do, it's work. In Cinderella stories, readers get to see drudgery and discomfort turn into acceptance and love. Also under this rubric are the stories of disguise and secret identity.

Historical: *The Runaway Princess* by Christina Dodd; *Scandal* by Amanda Quick; *Reader and Raelynx* by Sharon Shinn (which is a fantasy novel, but also a romance: that the transforming character is male doesn't mean it doesn't belong in this category).

Contemporary: *First Lady* by Susan Elizabeth Phillips; *The Winning Hand* by Nora Roberts; *Nine Coaches Waiting* by Mary Stewart.

Sleeping Beauty I have a sneaking fondness for stories of awakening. Not from sleep, of course, but those in which a character comes into her own, ie: 'wakes up' to a sense of her own potential and abilities. These characters discover and revel in new skills, or redevelop old ones. They try new experiences, make new friends, and change their own lives for the better. Change isn't alwasy easy. Sometimes it's a detonation in their existence. And sometimes they simply learn to let go of weight and pain carried too long. However it happens, these are the stories of lives refreshed and made wonderful.

Historical: *A Summer to Remember* by Mary Balogh; *Paladin of Souls* by Lois McMaster Bujold; *Guilty Pleasures* by Laura Lee Gurhke.

Contemporary: *Fast Women* by Jennifer Crusie; *Marianna* by Susannah Kearsley; *Lazarus Rising* by Anne Stuart.

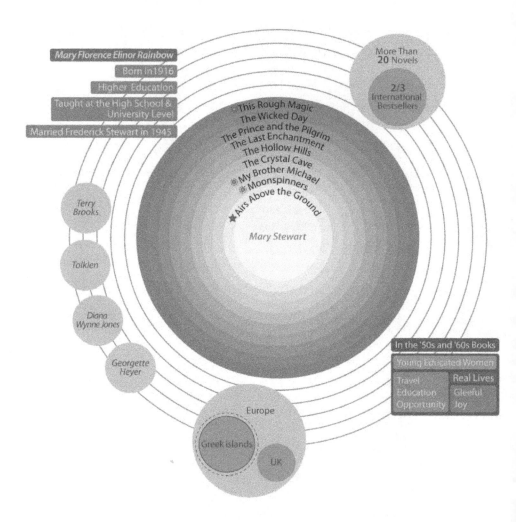

Mary Florence Elinor Rainbow
Born in 1916
Higher Education
Taught at the High School & University Level
Married Frederick Stewart in 1945

More Than **20** Novels

2/3 International Bestsellers

This Rough Magic
The Wicked Day
The Prince and the Pilgrim
The Last Enchantment
The Hollow Hills
The Crystal Cave
My Brother Michael
Moonspinners
Airs Above the Ground

Mary Stewart

Terry Brooks

Tolkien

Diana Wynne Jones

Georgette Heyer

In the '50s and '60s Books
Young Educated Women
Travel   Real Lives
Education   Gleeful
Opportunity   Joy

Europe

Greek islands

UK

Mary, Queen of Hearts

Despite being a rapacious reader of just about everything, during my formative years I managed to miss any number of writers who are the bedrock of their particular genres. For instance, I read Terry Brooks long before Tolkien (and yes, I'm aware of the gravity of that mistake). I didn't discover Diana Wynne Jones until my mid-twenties, around the same time I found Georgette Heyer. Another standard bearer I missed during my younger years, one who had a huge impact on many romance writers who followed her, is Mary Stewart.

Born in 1916, Mary Florence Elinor Rainbow was a trendsetter in many ways. In time when highter education was possible for women, though not extremely common, she received her BA in 1938, and her MA in 1941. She was an Observer during WWII, and for many years taught at the high school and university level. She married Frederick Stewart in 1945, and shortly after that, began to pursue writing as a serious career.

She wrote more than twenty novels, more than two-thirds of which were huge international best-sellers. Not all were romance, or romantic suspense, as they would be called today (ie: romances that are also mysteries). In fact, Stewart is almost even more famous for her Arthurian saga, which consists of *The Crystal Cave*, *The Hollow Hills*, *The Last Enchantment*, and *The Wicked Day*. She followed those four up much later with *The Prince and the Pilgrim*. Oddly enough, though I love Stewart's work, I've never read any of those. I run a fantasy and science-fiction specialty bookstore, and had to ban all things Arthur years ago for the sake of my sanity. But if I ever come out from behind that barricade, Stewart's take on the Matter of Britain will be what I turn to first.

The books I love best are the ones Stewart wrote in the '50s and '60s. They tend to be about young(ish) educated women, who are out making their ways in the world. Her heroines all have real lives: they have bills to pay, they're interested in travel, education and opportunity. But one of Stewart's strongest skills is her ability to capture atmosphere. She herself was one of those women, and it's evident. A thorough understanding and acceptance of the daily privations of life in post-war England runs through her early works, and with it, the sense of gleeful joy when those privations are eased.

Several of Stewart's books are set in the UK, but others are set across the wider European stage. A few take place in the Greek islands, and though some of her ruminations on the nature of the immutable 'Greek character' would cause fits in students of post-colonial post-modernism, she has a near perfect touch with description. When I discovered Stewart, I was not long returned from an extended stay in the Greek Islands, and reading *This Rough Magic*, *My Brother Michael*, and *Moonspinners* instantly transported me back. *Moonspinners*, by the way, was made into a movie. Sadly, the studio was Disney, and the film stars Hayley Mills, so I haven't quite worked up the nerve to watch it.

I find it very difficult to choose a favourite among Stewart's novels, but *Airs Above the Ground* is a perennial front-runner. Drugs, spies, a travelling circus, and the fabulous Lipizzan horses of the famed Spanish Riding School all come together in a delightful road-trip of a tale through rural Austria. It's also an unusal book in that the heroine has sex. Okay, yes, with her husband, and it happens off the page, but still! It marks a distinct departure from the strictures of the times. Stewart certainly wasn't the first person to put sex in her books, but she normalized it. Even more importantly, without graphic of explicit language, she made sex mutually enjoyable.

Mary Stewart epitomizes the voice of her generation: educated, thoughtful and forthright, with the sense of being both forward-looked and aware of the past that is particular of those who lived through WWII. The fantastically pulp nature of her cove art is a brilliant contrast to the deliciously crisp nature of her prose. For millions of readers, many of whom went on to become writers, she opened up the world.

I Want My Mummy

I'm a total chicken. This means I don't watch anything that smacks of horror: in fact, I tend to close my eyes when the music gets even a little bit ominous. It's not the gore I mind so much (though really, intestines belong on the *inside*), but the terror. The supposed cathartic release of the horror movie escapes me: I scare really easily, and unfortunately, I stay scared long after the movie ends. Which means I've missed any number of important genre movies: *The Thing*, *The Exorcist*, most of *Alien*. So imagine my joy when awkward first date manners had me agreeing to watch *The Mummy* remake.

Yeah. The date went about as well as you'd expect, but it did leave me with one consolation. Much to my surprise, I *loved* the movie. Some of that might have been relief: here was a remade horror movie that wasn't horror at all. Instead, it was action and comedy. But later, I realized that much of what I liked about *The Mummy* was in fact what I like about romance novels. I'm not alone in this, romance writers and readers tend to adore the movie. Here are a few reasons why, beyond the inevitable pairing of Rick and Evie.

1. It has a happy ending. And not a horror-movie happy ending, where a single character survives the devastation. In this case, Rick, Evie and Jonathan don't just survive, they emerge triumphant: alive, having soundly defeated the bad guys, and heading off to Cairo with saddlebags full of treasure. Even Ardeth, the Magi, survives. Apparently he wasn't originally supposed to, but the director liked actor Oded Fehr so much his part was rewritten to keep him onscreen. On behalf of myself and the rest of the film's fans, I can only say: thank goodness.

2. Happy endings require sacrifice. In the final action sequence, everyone has to sacrifice something he or she holds dear. Evie sacrifices knowledge and education when she abandons the golden book that has been her life's pursuit. Jonathan sacrifices his longed-for material wealth when he passes up on his chance to loot the treasure chamber. Rick... well, Rick has to give up the notion that he can save everyone. In order to save those who are most important, he has to stop trying to save Benny. And Benny, who is both bad guy minion and comic relief, gets Evie's long promised comeuppance.

3. It's replete with male heroic archetypes. First there's Rick. Played by Brendan Fraser, he's amusing, brawny, loyal and capable. The classic Adventurer Hero: not overly complicated, perhaps, but when the situation calls for dynamite, simple is usually the best choice. Then there's Ardeth Bey, played by Oded Fehr. He's a great example of the Mystical Hero: he shows up unexpectedly, he gives cryptic warnings, and has dark connections to an ancient magic. And of course, there's Imhotep himself. Arnold Vosloo plays the titular character as a Tortured Hero: desperate to make amends for the damage his past mistakes cost the woman he loves. He's also the villian, which makes things interesting, but more about that in a moment.

4. It features a functioning family. Which consists of only a brother and sister, but from the moment the inimitable John Hannah pops out of a sarcophagus to startle Rachel Weisz, they seem like real siblings. When in consequence she smacks his face as she helps climb out, I thought, 'Yeah, I'd do that.' Jonathan may disappoint Evie with his drinking and his gambling, but she listens to what he has to say. Evie may irritate Jonathan with her primness and erudition, but he feels for her when her job application is rejected yet again. They bicker constantly, and they enjoy needling one another, but they always, always have each other's backs.

5. The driving force of the plot is a love story. And no, that doesn't mean Evie and Rick. In this case, the primary love story is Imhotep's own. Think about it. The movie opens with the doomed and desperate romance between Imhotep and Anuk-su-namun. She's willing to give everything for the chance that they can be together: she even takes her own life. And despite being tortured and cursed—and dead for almost three thousand years—Imhotep struggles to be worthy of her belief in him. Everything that follows happens because he's desperate to revive her. He doesn't take over the world for his own sake, but for hers. All of his horrific actions: the murders, the plagues, the mind-enslavement; these are mere by-products of his ultimate goal, which is to bring his dead girlfriend back to life. Now *that's* romantic dedication. Sick and twisted and wrong? Definitely. But it gives emotional oomph to a popcorn spectacular.

Everybody's Hero

The Harry Potter books are an oddity in the book world. Not just because they sell so well, but because of how they sell, or rather, when. Each book has a strangely limited shelf life. Rowling's newest title might sell three-quarters of a million copies in twenty-four hours, but then, well, it's pretty much over. Sales rapidly fall off the map. Each of her books is the Best-Selling! Book! Evar!, but only for about a week. Every other week, every other day, the best-selling author in the world is Nora Roberts.[1]

Some of that is sheer logistics. Backlist is what truly powers an author's career. Rowling has seven novels and a couple of chapbook style reference works. As I write this, Nora has more than 175 titles in print, and the gods alone know how many reprint. The real estate she occupies in terms of shelf space is truly extraordinary. There are so many reissues, repackages and omnibus editions of her work that her publishers brand each previously unpublished title with a stylized 'NR' so her legions of readers will know what's actually new.

And those readers still have a lot to choose from. Roberts usually has five or six *new* titles each year. That number used to be higher, seven, eight, even nine, but in the late nineties, Nora stopped writing category romances ('category' is an industry term for line novels, like those of Mills & Boon, Harlequin and Silhouette). Nora was, in fact, one of the primary reasons for the success of Silhouette Books, which began as a category imprint of Simon & Schuster. After the bloody publishing house wars of the mid-eighties, Harlequin emerged triumphant as the owner of all three, but kept the Silhouette lines as a separate imprint within their romance empire. Roberts continued to write for Silhouette throughout those years, even as she branched off into writing longer, more mainstream titles for Bantam. Eventually, she moved to Putnam where, in the words of my Putnam rep, she finally found an editor who could keep up with her.

The story of Nora's start is well known in romance circles, and loved with fairy-tale familiarity. It's also vintage Nora. At the time, Roberts was a young single mother with two small and energetic sons. Trapped indoors by a blizzard that kept school cancelled for days, her only respite was the writing break she allowed herself in the afternoons. The boys were told not to interrupt unless there was fire or blood... spurting arterial blood, to be specific. Practicality, humour and hard work: these are some of the reasons Roberts was an is such a huge success. It took a few tries and several manuscripts, but in 1981, *Irish Thoroughbred* was published by Silhouette, and and a publishing legend was born.

Sounds melodramatic, eh? 'Legend'. But it's true. In the publishing world, Nora Roberts is Babe Ruth and Wayne Gretzky combined. She has won every award in the field multiple times. She's had more books on the New York Times list than any other author, in the number one spot, no less. She was a founding member of the Romance Writers of America, and the first person inducted into the Romance Writers Hall of Fame. Last year alone, four of her books were made into movies for the Lifetime Channel, and earlier this year, on Time Magazine's list of the top 100 Artists and Entertainers, Nora was #7.

Her stratospheric career has not been entirely free from strife. Janet Dailey, herself a successful romance novelist, inexplicably plagiarized one of Roberts' novels. When the plagiarism was discovered, Nora sued and won. But she didn't dwell, and she wasn't vindictive. She donatd the settlement to a literacy foundation, and moved on.

The wellspring of Nora's creativity is grounded by a work ethic of pure steel. Her book tour schedules read like a Spartan death march: TV spot at 6am, radio at 7am, warehouse by 8am to sign a thousand copies of the new hardcover, then off to the bookstore for noon... and it goes on like that for weeks. But tours aside, she doesn't live the jet-set lifestyle. Her family is her centre, and besides, she always has more stories to tell. Well-grounded, well-liked by her collegues, and well-loved by her fans: that's Nora Roberts.

1 http://www.noraroberts.com

I Got 99 Problems but a Bitch Ain't One

Sarah Wendell and Candy Tan occupy some interesting real estate in the romance world; a previously untenanted corner of Innernet and Romancelandia. *Smart Bitches, Trashy Books*[1] is a different sort of headspace: frank, forthright, and not above fart jokes. They not only review romance novels, but also subject them to analysis, and praise or pan as the situation requires. They demonstrate an unquenchable and exuberant love for the entire genre, while acknowledging—and even celebrating—its most ridiculous excesses. They've also popularized the ever-useful phrase 'man-titty' as a descriptive aid in the discussion of cover art. And now the original Smart Bitches have written a book of their own: *Beyond Heaving Bosoms: The Smart Bitches' Guide to Romance Novels*.

Jenny Crusie sums it up perfectly in her back cover quote: "I love the Smart Bitches. They look at romance with clear but loving eyes, and they do it with wit, style, intelligence, and snark". Yes, to all of that. *Beyond Heaving Bosoms* isn't a defense: the genre doesn't need one. Nor is it a textbook filled with critical application, or a list of good reads. Instead it's a cheerful guide to the best—and worst—the genre has to offer.

The Table of Contents is fully indicative of the Smart Bitches style and approach. The chapters aren't numbered, they're named. Chapter Cleavage, for instance, is the introduction. Chapter Corset focuses on heroines, and Chapter Codpiece on the heroes. Tan and Wendell mix their historical examination with healthy (even heaping) doses of humour. They track the overall change in the genre from Old Skool (1972 to the mid-'80s) to New Skool (early '80s to today). And they do it not from a distant academic perspective, but as passionately invested readers. The kind of fan who will pay outrageous prices for floor seats... but who will also boo and throw popcorn if the team (or in this case writer) doesn't bring it.

I can't quite tell how *Beyond Heaving Bosoms* would work for those unfamiliar with the genre. It's full of references and allusions that resonate more strongly if you have the kind of familiarity that comes from decades of reading. For me, that added a warm sense of collegiality. Though despite being an insider, I disagree with some of their conclusions about the nature of characters, and of stories themselves. But I enjoyed following the path they took to get there. And as Wendell and Tan make very clear, it doesn't matter. There is room for as many kinds of interpretation as there is overexposed vampire angst.

My favourite part of the book was also the most serious. It's a subsection of Chapter Phallus, titled "Controversies, Scandals, and Not Being Nice". It's the section in which Wendell and Tan expose some of the ugly arguments that happen offstage, between readers, writers, and the Romance world in general. Frankly, I think it should be required reading for writers, publishers, booksellers, and readers too, because the questions they raise are important. Should Black Romances be shelved with Romance or in the Black Authors section?* Many readers want to see the Black Authors section grow; many writers want access to the immense selling power of the Romance section. The question of gays in Romance is even more fraught: several years ago a particularly fearful RWA Board tried to pass a motion that would declare all Romances to be "between a man and a woman". So what does it mean that most of the people writing—and reading—gay e-romances are straight women?

The section on plagiarism didn't raise questions for me, except of the "What's *wrong* with you?" variety. In December 2007, a friend of Tan's discovered that novelist Cassie Edwards had been lifting passages from other works for years. Tan posted those findings, along with the response of Edwards' then-publisher Signet Books, and ignited a firestorm of truly epic proportions. What surprised, and disappointed, the Bitches most was how many responders attacked them for 'picking on' Edwards. Yes, they had often made fun of Edwards' books on the site. But plagiarism is wrong, no matter how long you've been doing it; how old you were when you started, and how Not Nice it is for a person to point out that you've been stealing someone else's words. Plagiarism is wrong. Period.

As I said, it was the most serious part of the book. I could have read twice as much. But Wendell and Tan play to their strengths, and one of those is a bawdy and irrepressable sense of humour. Sometimes that grated a little. The first mention of the hero's Wang of Mighty Loving is funny. The tenth? Not so much. But one of their more outrageous exclaimations made me laugh so hard on the subway that someone asked if I was okay. And isn't that what you want from your non-fiction? Fearless, insightful, and passionately devoted to the genre, Sarah Wendell and Candy Tan are very Smart Bitches indeed.

*This may be of those issues in which you realize things really are different in Canada (or at least in Toronto, where I checked several bookstores). In each store Romances were shelved in the Romance section, no matter the colour of the cover model's skin. Though four bookstore don't exactly constitute a scientific survey: your mileage may vary.

1 http://www.smartbitchestrashybooks.com

Love, Pain, and the Whole Damn Thing

Oprah's Book Club had a massive impact on the literary landscape, and I mean that in a good , non-dinosaur-killing way. The huge surge in the trade paperback market owes much to Oprah. I was working for Chapters when the whole thing got started, and the number of times *every day* we were asked for "that book Oprah was talking about" was mind-boggling. The only question asked nearly as often was "Why does she always choose such #&!% depressing books?"

Oprah does like tales of misery, of tragedy and despair: I won't presume to guess why. I do know that she was asked once why she never chose something positive for her book club, like a romance novel. She responded, somewhat scornfully, that no one read them. Her audience immediately corrected her. Surprised, she put the question up on her website, asking readers to name the genres of books they read most. Romance outnumbered every other category *combined*. Which wasn't surprise to anyone who works in the publishing industry, but after that, some other kinds of books began to make their way into Oprah's club. Of course since that brought Dr. Phil to prominence, maybe that wasn't such a good thing.

But Dr. Phil, smarm-master that he is, isn't the point. The point is that Oprah never felt that there was enough misery in romance novels. She could not equate them in her mind with the stories of desperate struggle that spoke to her most profoundly. She didn't believe they could encompass tragedy *and* a happy ending.

Which leads me to believe she hasn't read Barbara Samuel.[1]

Barbara Samuel is one of those rare people who wanted to be a writer all her life, and who actually succeeded at that aim. She put herself through university on writing scholarships, and afterwards wrote non-fiction to support herself as she made a name for herself in fiction. Although at least to start, it wasn't her own name. When she first began to work with Harlequin, the publisher kept the rights to the author's name. So she wrote her complex and engaging category novels under the pseudonym Ruth Wind. Later, as she branched out in to longer works, first historicals, then contemporaries, she used her own name, Barbara Samuel.

Under those names, and her newest, Barbara O'Neal, she has published almost 30 books. Those books have collected between them a remarkable number of awards, including five RITAs. Her success is due largely to the nuanced richness of her characters, but also to the complexity of the worlds they inhabit. When she writes historical fiction set in England, the religious bigotry of the time is not glossed over. If she writes a contemporary set in the United States, racial tensions are acknowledged—as is the realization that 'black' and 'white' are not the only races. In fact, her books often featured inter-racial relationships before those became a subcategory of their own.

If there's once thing Samuel understands, it's that no real life is free from catastrophe. And sometimes, they are of our own making. Her 2003 title, *A Piece of Heaven*, is an excellent illustration. It is the story of Luna McGraw and Thomas Coyote, who meet when she helps his grandmother out of a burning house (it's less melodramatic than it sounds). Both of them have been through some terrible times. Luna began to drink when her marriage collapsed, and ended by wrecking several cars, her career, and losing custody of her eight year old daughter. That daughter, now sixteen, is coming to stay for a year, and Luna, who has done the very hard work of putting herself back together, doesn't have room in her life for any distractions. Enter Thomas, whose desire for a family was doubly blighted when he found out he was sterile, and his wife left him for his brother. He is man whose door is open to strays, human and otherwise, but whose heart is heavily guarded. Neither of them is looking to get involved. But once they meet, all their earlier plans are thrown into colourful disarray.

There are other characters of course, all of whom are reeling under some kind of damage. There's a teenage neighbor trying to cope with the death of her father, a woman dealing with the loss of a husband who abandoned her years ago, a man trying to end a toxic relationship with his wife. As a former social worker, I usually have zero patience for addictions or abuse in my fiction, often because they bear no resemblance to the reality. *A Piece of Heaven* has both, and I couldn't put it down. Because Samuel not only did it right, she made it *matter*.

Samuel knows that tragedy doesn't have to be enormous. It can be devastatingly personal. Which makes sense: while we empathize with grand scale disasters, we *connect* best with personal tragedies. The kind that make you catch your breath because they're so immediate and comprehensible. Her characters are all of them survivors, of loss, of pain, of heartbreak. And they manage to move past those hurts. Not forget, or 'get over': move past. They earn the grace of their happy ending.

Which, more than anything else, is what Samuel wants to do. She is interested in survivors, in how people make it through terrible events and yet still manage to go on to lead full, powerful, joyful lives. The trauma is always going to be there: the joy can be there too.

Maybe someone should tell Oprah.

1 http://www.barbarasamuel.com

We Need to Talk

I've put it off long enough. Thought, 'We can get into that later', and 'I should wait till the fuss dies down a little'. But truth is, we're overdue. It's time we talked.

About *Twilight*.

(Don't groan. At least, not till we're done).

The talk has two parts. The first, about *Twilight*-the-novel, is fairly straightforward. I'm in the book business, and had seen the pre-publicity buzz turn into a roar. I read the book because I wanted to know what kind of tidal wave was headed my way. Afterwards, I thought it was: A) nothing new or exciting on the romance front; B) nothing new or exciting on the vampire front; and C) probably going to sell in huge quantities, though not necessarily out of my store.

I still stand by those conclusions. When it comes to romance (and vampires, for that matter), I don't care for melodrama, and have little patience for angst. *Twilight* is stuffed impossibly full of both. I found it readable, but far too self-absorbed to want to pick up the rest of the books in the series.

However...

That I didn't care for the interaction between Bella and Edward doesn't mean I think *Twilight*-the-phenomenon lacks an important and valuable love story. It's just that I think that love story that matters is the one between the readers and the books.

That's the second part, and it's big. Around the world, readers are truly connecting to the *Twilight* series. They're passionately attached to the story. I'm not talking about shrieking fangirls here, or anyone in a 'Team Jacob' T-shirt: I'm talking about *readers*. Millions upon millions upon millions of people loving *books*.

Everybody should have the chance to love a book that much. Because that kind of love really does bridge time and space. When you love a book with everything that is in you, that love lasts. If you pick it up again years later, decades, whatever, you may find the words no longer have the same music, or the story the same grandeur. But the *love*... that will still exist.

The immediacy of that tie is astonishing and powerful. There are books I only have to touch to be transported into a different era of my life: one in which I'm under foreign sky, perhaps; or in the company of someone I've since lost. I'm not the person I was when I first read those books—which is probably a good thing—but for a moment, I can remember how that person *felt*.

Did I say powerful? That's *primordial*.

Twilight also has the added bonus of being set in adolescence, that period in which so many of us first experience the fiery, dizzying rush of infatuation. When I saw the movie with a group of friends, we laughed aloud when Edward first swaggered into frame. That garnered us some vicious glares, but we weren't making fun. At least, not of the movie. If we'd been fourteen when these books came out, we likely would have thought Edward absolutely wonderful. Really, we were looking back in time, and laughing at our fourteen year old selves. Not unkindly, either.

Though it's not just teenagers reading the books. Nor is it just women. Though my bookstore isn't a representative example, the ratio of female *Twilight* buyers to male is about 80:20. Which is pretty good when you consider that women buy almost 80% of *all* books. Just before *Eclipse* (the third book in the series) arrived in paperback, I had a customer rush in looking for it. When told that the paperback release was just a few weeks away, he confessed that he was going to break his never-buy-hardcover policy. He *needed* the book. Now. He simply could not wait to find out what happened next.

When I asked, he couldn't quite pinpoint exactly what drew him so deeply to the story, only that he was drawn. I wondered if the vampire angle made it possible for him to move the book mentally out of the 'romance' category into the 'fantasy' category, but he went on to say that he loved the love story. He loved all of it. He just didn't know why.

Maybe his younger self knows. Maybe yours does too.

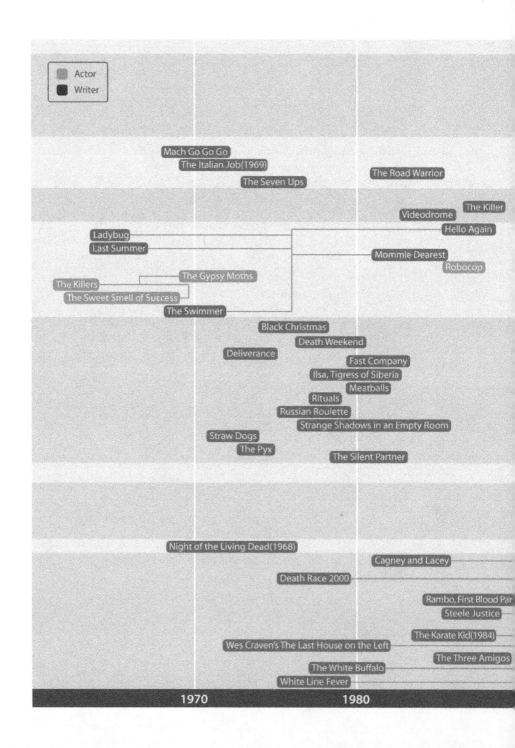

MOVIES

Ian Driscoll

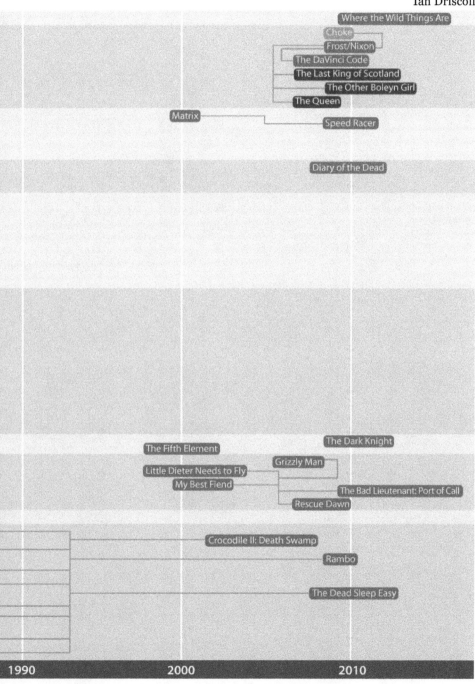

Where the Wild Things Are
Choke
Frost/Nixon
The DaVinci Code
The Last King of Scotland
The Other Boleyn Girl
The Queen
Matrix
Speed Racer
Diary of the Dead
The Dark Knight
The Fifth Element
Grizzly Man
Little Dieter Needs to Fly
My Best Fiend
The Bad Lieutenant: Port of Call
Rescue Dawn
Crocodile II: Death Swamp
Rambo
The Dead Sleep Easy

1990   2000   2010

Maurice Sendak!
I'm With You In Rockland

Spike Jonze's adaptation of Maurice Sendak's *Where the Wild Things Are* is not, thank god, a film about growing up.

Its opening credits, in which hand-scrawled monsters devour corporate logos, and its glorious freeze-frame opening title (hand-lettered against a smeared image of protagonist Max thundering down the stairs, fork in hand, in pursuit of his dog) announce that this is a film about childhood.

And *Where the Wild Things Are* is a film that's smart enough to understand that childhood is scary. It can be as cruel as it is joyful and as senseless as it is wondrous. And often, these contradictions occur because the world of childhood bangs up against the world of adults.

Working with the omnipresent Dave Eggers (if he didn't write the book you're reading, he wrote the introduction, or at least provided a blurb for the back cover), Jonze perfectly evokes childhood situations and emotions—and their friction with the realm of grownups.

In an early scene, Max has built an "igloo"—a tunnel in a snow bank—and tries to show it off to his older sister, who, busy talking on the phone, tells him to go play with his friends. From his lack of response or movement, from the way he stands on tip-toe, peering through the window at his sister, it's clear that he doesn't have any. In an attempt to connect with her, Max instigates a snowball fight with his sister and her friends—a fight that ends with Max's snow fort collapsed on top of him, and Max in tears. Childhood play runs smack up against the adult (or at least adolescent) world, and it hurts.

The snowball fight/fort incident later become a heroic tale in Max's retelling, and finds a happier resolution when Max, having run away from home and ended up on the island of Wild Things, organizes them to build the ultimate fort. It also finds an analogue when Max, playing king of the Wild Things, divides them into teams (good guys and bad guys) for a dirt clod war. (If you're not familiar, it's a melee in which people pelt one another with, well, clods of dirt. It's actually a pretty awesome part of childhood.) Predictably, participants get hurt, get hit when it's "not fair," and storm off, sulking. But in this case, it's Max, in the adult-responsibility role of king, who's to blame for the hurt and tears.

Of course, Max is not the first to bring adult concerns to the land of the Wild Things. (Who, it turns out, have names. Apparently, when the book was being adapted for an opera, Sendak named them after his relatives. They've been renamed for the film.)

Even before he arrives, the Wild Things have relationship issues. Personal issues. Interpersonal issues. Perhaps even psychological issues. Many of them mirror Max's own problems: like Carol, he has trouble controlling his anger; like Alexander, he wants to be noticed; like Judith, he is bossy; like Ira, he is clingy; like Douglas, he desperately wants friends; like The Bull, he is worried what people think of him. And like KW - ?

Is KW some part of Max? If she is, it's not a part of him that I can readily identify. Is she representative of his sister, who ignores him to spend with her friends, or his mother, who's dating Mark Ruffalo?

It's around KW that the simple metaphor of the Wild Things as representatives of aspects of Max's personality breaks down. And I think this is purposeful. The film isn't legible in simply Freudian terms. Childhood is not about metaphors. It's about experience.

Throughout the film, we encounter other discordant elements—animals that, while in the land of the Wild Things, are not themselves wild. There's a housecat. An improbably large dog ("Oh, it's that dog. Don't feed it, he'll just follow you around"). And a raccoon, an animal that straddles the wild/tame divide.

What are these animals doing in the land of the Wild Things?

I think we get the answer to that question when, at one point, we meet the raccoon inside one of the Wild Things (where Max is hiding, from one of the other Wild Things). The promotional campaign for *Where the Wild Things Are* claims that inside all of us is a wild thing. But it seems that inside every Wild Thing is also a domesticated thing. Inside every child, not to put too fine a point on it, is an adult.

But thankfully, we don't see adult Max, because, as I said earlier, this is not a film about growing up. In the end, Max solves his problems by not solving them. Why? Because he's a kid. So he runs away again, but this time he runs away to home, there to find waiting for him soup, and chocolate cake, and his mother, not hysterical, just happy to see him. She sits and watches him eat, and the expression on her face seems to quote Ginsberg:

> *I'm with you in Rockland*
> *in my dreams you walk dripping*
> *from a sea-journey on the highway*
> *across America in tears*
> *to the door of my cottage in the Western night*

The Wild Things have issues, yes. But they talk around instead of about them. Instead of discussing, like adults, they throw dirt clods and knock down trees and build forts and lash out and run and hope. Perhaps it's because they lack the vocabulary.

Or maybe it's simply because they know that sometimes, it's better just to howl.

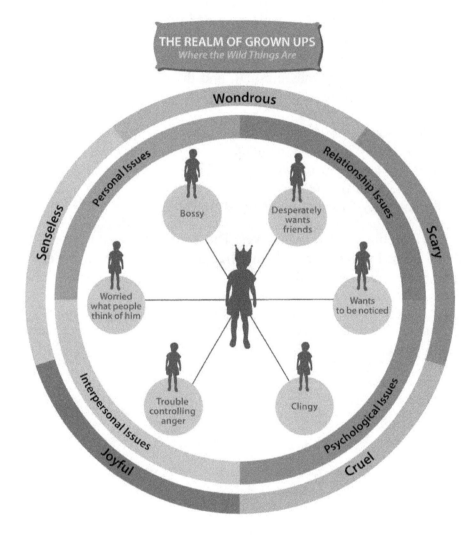

Is This What You Call A Dachshund?

Normally, I think of Ron Howard as the Midas of mediocrity – everything he touches turns to boring. So, what went right with *Frost/Nixon*?

(If you're totally unaware of the last 40 years of American history, spoiler alert.)

There's a moment near the end of the *Frost/Nixon* in which Frank Langella's Nixon, shaken from his trailer-worthy excited utterance ("I'm saying that when the President does it, that means it's not illegal!"), stumbles out of the house in which the interview has been taking place. Outside is a crowd, which we have seen him glad-hand his way through numerous times by this point. But in the wake of his disastrous final interview, the equation is changed. Tricky Dick is out of tricks. He's surrounded, seeing himself as he's seen. Fumbling for a safe interaction, he approaches a woman standing on the sidewalk with her dog and asks, as if unsure of the answer, "Is this what you call a dachshund?" The woman proffers the dog and, his fingers curled into loose, arthritic claws, Nixon skritches the animal gently on the head.

It's not a stretch to see a reference to/mirroring of Nixon's famous Checkers speech, but this is not a moment of misdirection or politicking; it's a moment of human vulnerability, where the only safe love is unconditional dog-love. Which is not to say that *Frost/Nixon* is, as some have claimed, an apologia for the Nixon administration and its unequivocal crimes. It's something more complex—and more equivocal.

Peter Morgan, who wrote the stage play *Frost/Nixon*, as well as also scripting and co-producing the screen adaptation, seems to have an uncanny knack for getting inside the private psychology of public figures in moments of crisis. (Not that he bats a thousand: he's also responsible for *The Last King of Scotland*, about which I'm pretty ambivalent, and *The Other Boleyn Girl*, a movie for which the term credits should be replaced with, "blames".) As an evocation of life under the sunlamp of hot media, Nixon's encounter with the dachshund is a mirror of Elizabeth II's encounter with the stag near the end of *The*

Queen (although an equally strong case for mirroring could be made for the scenes of Nixon staring out over the ocean in the film's coda). These are ambiguous moments that force the audience to project and draw their own conclusions, and in so doing, confront the fact that we may not know as much as we assume—that sound bites, scrums or indeed a person's professional conduct may not tell the whole story.

Hollywood in general (and Ron Howard in particular) isn't very good with ambiguity (exhibit A: the frankly insulting *The DaVinci Code*, where the only thing ambiguous is the motivation behind Tom Hanks' hair cut). But the Nixon story is all about ambiguity and plausible deniability the dark matter of what could have been contained in the missing 18 minutes of White House tape. Interestingly, one of *Frost/Nixon*'s most debate-worthy sequences involves a telephone call from Nixon to Frost that Nixon later can't recall, and which effectively gives him his own missing 18 minutes. Is unrecorded experience real? Discuss.

Frost/Nixon is a story with an unstable footing, a story of changing media changing the world, a story of the power of the television camera as much as the power of men of power (all that on top of being, in itself, an echo-chamber adaptation of an adaptation of media event). As Sam Rockwell (redeeming himself slightly for the execrable *Choke* in the role of James Reston, Jr.) summarizes:

> You know the first and greatest sin of the deception of
> television is that it simplifies; it diminishes great, complex
> ideas, trenches of time; whole careers become reduced to
> a single snapshot. At first I couldn't understand why Bob
> Zelnick was quite as euphoric as he was after the interviews,
> or why John Birt felt moved to strip naked and rush into the
> ocean to celebrate. But that was before I really understood
> the reductive power of the close-up, because David had
> succeeded on that final day, in getting for a fleeting moment
> what no investigative journalist, no state prosecutor, no
> judiciary committee or political enemy had managed to get;
> Richard Nixon's face swollen and ravaged by loneliness,
> self-loathing and defeat. The rest of the project and its
> failings would not only be forgotten, they would totally cease
> to exist.

Reston's words resonate today (think of the Bush White House's stridently reductive soundbiting of the good/evil dichotomy). But *Frost/Nixon* is not about good or evil. It's not about private or public. It's not even about Frost or Nixon.

It's about that slash.

I'm willing to argue that *Frost/Nixon* may be the world's first Oscar-nominated slash fiction (tell you what; instead of delving into an almost-certainly NSFW explanation, I'll let you Google that if necessary). The slash is where things brush up against one another. It's not a reconciliation of opposites, or an equalization of quantities. It's not umbilical or connective. At best, it's an imperfect equation, a division with a remainder.

And perhaps what remains is Nixon the man. Not that that's a simple thing – as a man, he's still a combination of opinion and fact, nature and nurture, paucity of foresight and surfeit of hindsight. And at the centre of it all is something untouched (and maybe untouchable). As Henry Kissinger put it when describing Nixon, "The essence of this man is loneliness."

To return to my initial question, what went right here may be the fact that *Frost/Nixon* doesn't choose between right and wrong for you. It asks you to think about complex ideas. And that's anything but boring.

Go!

I recently had a chance to watch the Wachowski siblings' live-action adaptation of Tatsuo Yoshida's *Speed Racer* (aka the much-more-evocative *Mach Go Go Go*) for a second time. After 135 hallucinatory, candy-coated minutes of Möbius strip racetracks and Möbius strip plot, I was left with one question: is this the future of cinema?

Speed Racer tosses linear narrative out the power window in its opening sequence, as it Tokyo drifts between an elementary-school-aged Speed Racer doodling flip-book racecars in class, a teenage Speed Racer racing against his brother's ghost (in his imagination) while redlining toward the checkered flag on a CGI racetrack that leaves Newtoninan physics in the rearview mirror, and a formative-years montage that gets gallons to the mile. It's a Pimp-My-Ride mission statement that says, in no uncertain terms: ADHD is not a learning disability. It's an evolutionary adaptation. In the space of a few minutes, Speed Racer traces the entire history of animation, then proceeds to colour outside the lines as it delineates the go-go-check world of tomorrow.

The world of *Speed Racer* moves too fast for physics. It's a world where cars pedal-to-the-metal at over 800 kph, racetracks look like rollercoasters and people age in jumpcuts, only accessing the intervening years through dramatically convenient, on-the-fly flashbacks. In *Speed Racer* (as in cinema, as in life), the only direction is forward.

This is a world where everyone has their own personal greenscreen, and every speech is accompanied by a background montage that illustrates, complements and amplifies what is spoken. It's the triumph of the subjective, as dialogue scenes become paired monologues become vehicles for a stream-of-consciousness motion-controlled cameras that no longer need a shot/reverse shot structure to tell you who's talking to whom. Case in point: as Speed Racer, his girlfriend Trixie (side note: I could watch Christina Ricci weld all day long; a previously unsuspected fetish) and Racer X drive through the mountains, each in their own car, a three-lane dialogue scene takes place. But instead of cutting between the speakers, the camera simply zooms and tracks in and out from one cockpit to the other, never missing a beat of the conversation.

It's a bravura sequence that leads to an even more bravura fight scene between the Racer family (Chim-Chim and all) and the agents of the requisite villainous racing tycoon, Arnold Royalton. The fight evolves the Wachowski's *Matrix* aesthetic in a way that its sequels failed so miserably to do, creating anime speed-lines out of swirls of snow through camera movements, using the fighters' bodies to wipe (again rather than cutting) from one struggle to another and perfectly tracking the fisticuffs among no fewer than a dozen combatants. All this with a swelling score that breaks out—at the perfect moment—into a rendition of the *Speed Racer* theme. It's something pretty rare, that scene—a moment of pure, cinematic joy.

But *Speed Racer* also has a serious chassis. Its plot driver is a story of big, corrupt, colluding business out to profit from or destroy the livelihoods of independents—people who do it for love—and in these times of (can't believe I'm going to type this, but here it goes) global economic crisis, it resonates—far moreso than the first time I watched the film.

Why didn't Speed Racer do better at the box office? Good movies often don't, but that's a Model-T answer. I think the real reason is that the people who buy the tickets just aren't ready for a movie that starts in overdrive and gears up from there. They're used to Michael Bay using special effects to make product placements look good. Or Spielberg using special effects to serve classic Hollywood storytelling models. In Speed Racer, the Wachowskis use special effects to serve storytelling models that have are barely off the assembly line. Speed Racer plays Chicken with the audience, and I think a lot of people yanked their aesthetic steering wheels to the right and ended up seeing little more than the Wachowski's brake lights disappearing in the rearview mirror.

So, yeah, *Speed Racer* is the newest entry into my list of favourite car chase movies. It might not deliver the visceral tension of *The Seven Ups* or the sustained adrenaline of *The Road Warrior* or the unrelenting inventiveness of *The Italian Job* (1969 version, as if I needed to clarify) or the creeping speedometer of suspense that is *Duel*.

What it does do is perfectly capture—and realize—the childhood dream of what it would be like to be a racecar driver. The cars of Speed Racer don't run on gas, or ethanol, or even hydrogen. They run on pure imagination.

Cool beans.

Dangerous Because
It Has A Philosophy

In David Cronenberg's *Videodrome*, shortly before the arrival of the least sexy waiter in the history of cinema (go rent the movie), Max Renn (James Woods) and Masha (Lynne Gorman) share the following exchange on the nature of the phantom Videodrome signal Renn is tracking:

MASHA
Videodrome is something for you to leave alone.
Videodrome. What you see on that show, it's for real.
It's not acting. It's snuff TV.

MAX RENN
I don't believe it.

MASHA
So, don't believe.

MAX RENN
Why do it for real? It's easier and safer to fake it.

MASHA
Because it has something that you don't have,
Max. It has a philosophy. And that is what makes it
dangerous.

That, in a nutshell, is how I feel about the Cultural Gutter. It's dangerous because it has a philosophy.

What are the tenets of that philosophy? I'm pretty sure it's post-po-mo, and believes we've gone beyond any sort of central or authoritative narrative (and contends that's really the central metaphor of *Diary of the Dead*). Yet at the same time it abhors aintitcoolnews.com's onanistic abuse of the exclamation point.

The Gutter would rather watch Turner Classic Movies than AMC, even though it's kind of creeped out by Ted Turner, because it believes movies are meant to be seen in their proper aspect ratio, and from beginning to end without commercial interruption. (It admires David Lynch for his stand on this, among other things.)

83

The Gutter went to shoot-along screenings of *The Killer* back in the 90s, and got that out of its system. Now, it makes an ominous half-turn to stare down people who talk during movies. It gets up and exits the cinema to complain if the film goes out of focus, or if the sound is bad. Insofar as this goes, the Gutter may be bit of a cranky old man. It definitely likes wearing cardigans, though part of this is in homage to Bob Newhart.

It's still kind of angry about the replacement of unionized projectionists with pimply-faced candy-bar staff. It believes the projectionist is the last member of the film crew, and the one with the most power.

It believes that even though the seventh art is a latecomer, it's still an art form.

And yeah, it kind of always wanted to French kiss a television.

So, why put yourself out there? Why write several hundred words a month? Why imagine your opinion matters to anyone, or that you have anything of value to contribute? Why do it for real, when it's easier and safer to fake it? Maybe simply because stuff can't be uncommunicated, and because a bullet in the right place can change the world, but it's no substitute for a good meme.

Or maybe because the battle for the mind of North America will be fought in the Gutter. The Gutter is the retina of the mind's eye. Therefore, the Gutter is part of the physical structure of the brain. Therefore, whatever appears on the Gutter emerges as raw experience for those who read it. Therefore, the Gutter is reality, and reality is less than the Gutter.

You could think on that. Or you could ignore this article entirely and watch the version of Videodrome Brian O'Blivion would watch—all the good bits[1]—in eight minutes and 29 seconds.

Either way, keep tuning in to The Cultural Gutter—the one you take to bed with you.

---

1 www.youtube.com/watch%3Fv%3DYtp69fBh0J8 (Will anyone really type this out, other than you?)

A Drowning Man

Tomorrow (November 7, if I post this on time), Toronto's Trash Palace[1] is showing a print of Frank Perry's *The Swimmer*. If you're in the city, do yourself a favour: go see it. If you're elsewhere (I understand the internets now extend beyond the GTA), do yourself a favour: go rent it.

Based on the John Cheever story of the same name, *The Swimmer* stars Burt Lancaster as Ned "Neddy" Merril, denizen of the affluent suburbs of Westchester. His diminutive nickname is a metanym, I think, for the entire film—the society being portrayed, the plot that unfolds and the man at the centre of it all. The false camaraderie it implies, the superficial bullet-point relationships and false-front (self) images unfold over the course of the film, until their weight overwhelms even the barrel-chested Lancaster.

But maybe I'm getting ahead of myself.

The premise of the movie is pretty simple, if unusual. As the film opens, Lancaster is at a pool/cocktail party at the Westerhazys'. When it comes time to leave, he hits upon a novel idea, which I'd perhaps best let him explain:

> NEDDY
> Well now, with the Grahams there's a string of pools that curves clear across the county to our house. Well look: the Grahams, the Lears, the Bunkers. Then over the ridge. Then a—portage through the Paston's riding ring to the—Hallorans and the Gilmartins. Then down Erewise Lane to the Biswangers, and then—Wait a minute, who's next? I can't think, I had it just a minute ago. Who is it? Well, who is it? Who's next to the Biswangers?
>
> HELEN WESTERHAZY
> Shirley Abbott.

NEDDY

Shirley Abbott. And across Route 424 to the
recreation center pool, and up the hill and I'm home.
Well don't you see? I just figured it out. If I take a
sort of a dogleg to the southwest... I can swim home.

Which is exactly what he does over the rest of the film's running time:
portage from backyard to backyard, pool to pool, swimming a length
in each. Along the way, things get a little weird.

Of course, you'd expect no less from director Frank Perry. Perry
also helmed such notable cum notorious flicks as *Ladybug, Ladybug*
(nuclear paranoia fabulism at its best), *Last Summer* (which is less
a loss-of-innocence story than an annihilation-of-innocence story),
Mommie Dearest (the first film to sweep the Razzies) and *Hello Again*
(zombie Shelly Long? Comedy gold!), among others. Along with his
collaborator and wife, screenwriter Eleanor Perry, he specialized in
peeling away the veneer of polite society (impolite society, too, come
to think of it) and showing his characters ugly things in beautiful ways.

The Swimmer definitely bears Perry's stamp, but according to the
interviews on Saturday Night at the Movies[2] (god bless you, Elwy
Yost), he left the production due to creative differences. Several
segments were re-shot after his departure, and a key scene, in which
Neddy meets with his former mistress, was reportedly actually
directed by an uncredited Sydney Pollack.

So, no support for auteur theory here. The Swimmer is definitely a team
effort. It's hard to go wrong with source material as strong as Cheever's
story, but a lot of credit definitely goes to Eleanor Perry. Cheever's
story covers fewer than 10 pages, and her 95-minute screenplay never
feels stretched or repetitive. If the short story is the most challenging
literary form, the feature film adaptation of a short story may very
well be the most challenging task a screenwriter can undertake.

Which brings us to Burt Lancaster (Side note: you must also see *The Killers, The Sweet Smell of Success* and *The Gypsy Moths*). Lancaster is a no-fooling movie star, and almost every inch of him is in display in The Swimmer, in which the sum total of his wardrobe is a pair of swim trunks. How much farther can he strip, when he's wearing nothing but a swimsuit? You'd be surprised.

Throughout the film, there are clues that things are not as they should be. Marigolds bloom out of season. People react strangely to ordinary topics of conversation, make seemingly incongruous offers and attack without apparent provocation. Pools are found dry and drained, houses for sale. It's later than you think, and things are breaking down.

But what communicates this breakdown most remarkably is Lancaster's physical acting in the film. (Side note two: I think physical acting is an underappreciated talent. Watch Peter Weller in the first two *Robocop* films, then watch anyone else play the part in any other *Robocop* franchise production; he's the only one with the physical acting talent to make *Robocop* believable. Addendum to side note two: don't watch *Robocop 2*, or any of the franchise's later productions.) He peels away at his character with a limp, a slouch, a slowing pace, a shiver and a less frequent and less credible smile. But it's not just a physical breakdown he's showing us—it's a mental, emotional and societal one as well.

It's a performance that hurts like a lungful of water, an evocation of what it feels like to go from swimming to drowning.

So, like I said, go see it.

1 trashpalace.ca
2 tvo.org/snam

Shameless And Greedy
People Of Dismal Taste

Interviewed about the legacy of Canadian tax shelter films in *Cinema Canada* in 1985, Mordecai Richler said,

> I think they squandered a grand opportunity and it's largely the fault of producers who were shameless and greedy, people of dismal taste, who were more interested in making deals than films and who made a lot of money for themselves. And so Canadian films do not enjoy a larger reputation anywhere and it's a pity... a lot of damage has been done.

Well, Mordecai, I couldn't disagree more.

In this era of Bill C-10 (which may be gone, but which leaves behind its ideological sediment), and $44.8-million in cuts to arts-and-culture programs (this in spite of a Conference Board of Canada report attesting to the economic benefits of investing in Canadian culture), I think it's more important than ever to remember and celebrate the genre exercises upon which our film industry—and the careers of some of its brightest stars—were built. My Canada includes sleazy movies.

But first, a little primer on the tax shelter years: Although the late 70s are regarded as the heyday of tax shelter films, a 60% tax write-off for investment in Canadian films was available from 1954 on. In 1975, Minister of Finance John Turner announced a new income tax regulation allowing "investors to deduct in one year, against income from all sources, 100% [!] of their investment in certified feature films." Moreover, it was retroactive, and included any film productions begun after Nov. 18, 1974. 100% tax-shelter financing more or less continued until 1982, when it fell prey to the vicious beast known as distribution. (The preceding is a gross oversimplification, but for the complete story on what was and could have been, read

Wyndham Wise's excellent and exhaustive article, "Canadian cinema from boom to bust: the tax-shelter years"[1], from which I've cribbed liberally.)

But by that point, the damage was done. We already had *Black Christmas. Meatballs. Fast Company. Ilsa, Tigress of Siberia. The Pyx.*

Russian Roulette. Strange Shadows in an Empty Room. And a host of others. Some have gone on to prestigious DVD releases or undeservedly painful remakes, but most moulder in VHS bins.

Recently (the day before Canada Day, as a matter of fact), I had the opportunity to see a trio of these hidden zirconia, and I have never felt such as swell of patriotism in my life.

The evening started with a screening of *The Silent Partner*, in which bank teller Elliott Gould preempts Christopher Plummer's scheme to rob his bank. Several double crosses and corpses later, Gould comes out on top, and along the way, we're treated to an early semi-dramatic turn by John Candy and the you-can't-unsee-it-once-you've-seen-it sight of Christopher Plummer not only in a mesh t-shirt, but also in drag. Written by Curtis Hanson and produced by Garth Drabinsky, *The Silent Partner* is easily one of the more entertaining crime dramas of the 70s, which is saying something.

Next up was *Rituals*, starring Hal Holbrook as one of five doctors who go on a fishing vacation deep in the Canadian wilderness only to discover that a crazed ex-patient is tracking them with murderous intent. The plot borrows heavily from *Deliverance*, but if anything, *Rituals* looks like it was far more hellish to make – for most of its running time, the actors trudge through forests and swamps, wet and filthy, surrounded by hordes of black flies that ain't CGI. If you can find a print where you can actually see the action (the one I saw was murky to say the least), give it watch. You won't be disappointed.

We rounded out the evening with *Death Weekend*. A Canadian *Straw Dogs, Death Weekend* is one of Ivan Reitman's earliest productions, and centres on the tribulations of couple who are attacked by a group of ruffians at their cottage. If you've seen *Straw Dogs*, you can figure out how it ends. It's not as shattering as Peckinpah's film, but it's satisfying, and smarter than expected.

But where are the midnight Canuxploitation screenings of tomorrow going to come from when funding for anything even remotely artsy is on the chopping block? Especially when there's no reasoning with the people holding the axe? As Tom McSorley, Executive Director of the Canadian Film Institute, recently observed, what lies behind the current government's arts funding cuts is "ideological adamant rock... I don't think they listen with any degree of interest to the fact that the economic impact of the arts is demonstrably positive."

Time has been kind to the tax shelter films. The opportunity wasn't as squandered as Mordecai Richler would have us believe. A lot of genuine entertainment, expression and—yes, I'll say it—art squeezed out between the lines of the producers' ledgers, and we're all richer for it. It would be great if today's filmmakers got the same chance. But in the current political climate, that's a big if.

I like to think that if Mordecai Richler were being interviewed today, he might use that descriptor—"shameless and greedy people of dismal taste"—to describe a group other than the producers of those dingy celluloid dreams.

I know I would.

1 http://findarticles.com/p/articles/mi_m0JSF/is_22_7/ai_30155873/

Having Your Duality And Eating It, Too

When the question arises of who could be the villain in a third Batman movie, I'm stymied. I can't picture The Penguin or The Riddler or Catwoman working in the world Christopher Nolan has created. Poison Ivy? I don't think so. The Mad Hatter? Clayface? Kite Man? Bane? Nope, nope, nope and please god no.

The only possible candidates I've come up with are Hugo Strange, Black Mask and possibly Deadshot (and, it goes without saying, the Gorilla Boss).

Why is it so hard to come up with a villain for a third Batman film? I think it's because *The Dark Knight* so effectively nullifies its own superheroic elements—and I'm not the first one to make note of this. As Christopher Bird of *Mightygodking*[1] observed in his one-sentence review:

> There are many reasons to see *The Dark Knight*, many of which have been repeated elsewhere many times over, but I will merely say this: any movie starring Christian Bale, Heath Ledger, Aaron Eckhart, Maggie Gyllenhaal, Michael Caine and Morgan Freeman which trusts one of its most powerful and emotional moments to Tiny Lister, and makes it work perfectly, is a movie that is a cut above.

Lister, best known for playing the president of the universe (bless your ludicrously self-indulgent soul, Luc Besson) in *The Fifth Element*, is indeed entrusted with one of the most important sequences in the film, and it does work—maybe too well. As Batman and The Joker battle it out atop the Gotham City skyline, the action intercuts with a sequence that brings the story crashing back down to sea level. The Joker, acolyte of chaos, has set up a variation on the classic prisoner's dilemma by putting bombs on two ferries: one filled with criminals and the other filled with average Gothamites. The catch: the detonator for each ferry is in the hands of the people on the other. The only sure way to save

93

yourself is to blow the other boat up. Then, at the crucial moment, prisoner Tiny Lister takes the detonator on his boat—and tosses it out the window.

What's remarkable about that sequence is that while it plays out the big clash-of-icons themes in the movie (The Joker's chaos unfolds, but backfires on him, as chaos is wont to do; figuratively, Two-Face's coin lands unscarred-side up, validating the morality of chance; good and evil define and demand one another), it also negates the entire superhero side of the plot.

The people of Gotham do what needs to be done and make the right decisions without so much as a pause to ask, WWBD? They save themselves while Batman is busy having a philosophical discussion with The Joker (the brilliantly not-even-remotely-subtle device of flipping the camera upside down for The Joker's half of that conversation underscores what has happened here: things have changed. As below, so above.)

That would be enough, but just as Tiny Lister steps up to fill the heroic role, another everyman steps into the key villain role. Because the biggest threat Batman faces in *The Dark Knight* isn't The Joker or Two-Face or his own inner demons, or even the big screen comeback of Anthony Michael Hall. His biggest threat in the film is an accountant.

There have been more than a few critics who have complained about the film's numerous and convoluted subplots, but the one featuring Joshua Harto as Wayne Enterprises employee Coleman Reese is perhaps the most interesting. Harto uncovers Wayne's secret identity not by trailing him to the Batcave or bugging the Batmobile or torturing Alfred, but through simple forensic accounting (in a plot that mirror's Batman's follow-the-money takedown of Chin Han's mob money launderer). Armed with this information, Harto can destroy Batman not in a grand rooftop battle or through a protracted war of ideologies (or by letting Frank Miller write him), but simply by going on television. And because he's going to do it during the day, Batman is powerless to stop him. So, who you gonna call? Bruce Wayne.

In what I think is one of the most inspired sequences in the film, Bruce Wayne manages to save Harto's life (in true playboy billionaire style, by crashing a Lambourghini), then looks Harto in the eyes – man to (not Bat) man. With nary a Batarang in sight, with just a traffic accident and a significant look, Bruce Wayne saves Batman.

Which may go a long way toward explaining why Christian Bale is credited not as Batman, or even Bruce Wayne/Batman, but as Bruce Wayne.

The Dark Knight is clearly obsessed with duality. With its layered internal and external conflicts between Bruce Wayne and Batman and The Joker and Harvey Dent/Two Face, a double-blind love triangle and multiple mirroring plots and sub plots, the film is gay for duality. The Joker's line, "You complete me," might just has well have been "I wish I could quit you." But it has its duality and eats it too.

Which ends up making for a surprisingly satisfying meal.

1 mightygodking.com (Pay special attention to his post on why he should write The Legion of Super Heroes. Especially if you work for DC Comics.)

His Soul's Still Dancing

In the course of making *The Bad Lieutenant: Port of Call—New Orleans*, Werner Herzog seems to have discovered the only way to save Nicolas Cage: let him drown.

Why am I writing about Nicolas Cage again, after effectively writing him off in a previous column?[1] Maybe because, with his ferocious performance in *TBL: POC-NO*, Cage has been resurrected for me.

It's a resurrection that happens onscreen as well as off. The film opens with the camera following a snake as it swims through what turns out to be a flooded precinct jail, where bad detectives Nic Cage and Val Kilmer are taking bets on how long it will take a man locked in one of the cells to drown. Cage eventually abandons the game, though, and jumps in to save the man, at which point the screen goes black.

We catch up with him again some months later, as he's being promoted from bad detective to bad lieutenant, primarily for saving the man's life. But he has emerged from the water wracked with chronic pain from the back injury he sustained jumping in—a staggering, lurching Frankenstein's monster, constantly holding one shoulder higher than the other (a crooked man, walking a crooked mile).

The allusion to Frankenstein is deliberate, and none too subtle. Cage's lieutenant is, like the monster, reanimated flesh. He is the walking dead.

And if there was ever a city in which to be a zombie, New Orleans is that city.

Herzog's New Orleans is a drowned city, and even years after Katrina, the (shore)line between land and water is blurry at best. Aquatic reptiles wander everywhere: into jails, as in the film's opening. Onto roads, as in the sequence where Cage visits the scene of an accident both caused and watched by alligators. And, inevitably, into Cage's mind, as in the stakeout sequence where he hallucinates lizards: "What the hell are those iguanas doing on my coffee table?"

This is a place where the dead dance. There's a sequence—the one that people walk away from the film (or even the trailer) quoting, in which Cage tricks a group of drug dealers into shooting a group of gangsters. When all the gangsters are down, Cage demands that the dealers shoot the lead gangster again. When asked, "What for?" he responds, punctuating his explanation with a gasping laugh: "His soul's still dancing!"

While the dealers are deciding what to do, we get to watch as the dead man breakdances around his own corpse. It's a mesmerizing scene, and in the film's voodoo-inflected setting, it doesn't even need Cage's uninterrupted drug abuse to seem plausible.

(Side note: I really wish that scene weren't in the trailer. It would have been great to stumble across it in the course of watching the film. It would have been a stunning discovery.)

Of course, because this is nominally a police procedural, with Cage investigating a murder, the film also places emphasis on people who speak for, and act on behalf of the dead. And in the course of the film, acting on behalf of the dead becomes an exercise in just plain acting.

Cage's performance in *TBL: POC-NO* is all about acting. That is to say, he's playing a character who's constantly acting, pretending, lying. He acts the part of a cop while being a crook. He acts the part of a crook while being a cop. He acts straight when high, dedicated when desperate, confident when utterly lost. He approaches everyone he encounters with a new face (if the same improbably hairline), and fools the audience enough to leave unanswered questions about where his loyalties lie. Is he undercover or under-undercover?

The point is that he never stops performing, within the film or for the camera. He does what it takes to become the bad man for Herzog's bad world.

And make no mistake: this is a bad world. It does not reward good behaviour. It does not spare the innocent. As Herzog himself put it in *Grizzly Man*: "I believe the common character of the universe is not harmony, but chaos, hostility, and murder."

Of course, like practically everything that comes out of Herzog's mouth, that's probably at least part exaggeration and part straight-faced joke. Truth be told, he's not really interested in the truth.

While he works in both narrative and documentary forms, he eschews the term "documentary," instead preferring to label his films "fiction" and "non-fiction." They're all stories, it's just that some of them are made up, and others aren't. Several of Herzog's films straddle the line, or get to be both: take a look at how his documentary *Little Dieter Needs to Fly* relates to its narrative remake *Rescue Dawn*, how the polygraph-buster that is *My Best Fiend* writes and rewrites personal history, or how *Grizzly Man* treats the comforting (and sometimes deadly) narratives/lies we tell ourselves.

All of which is to say that, yes, the common character of the universe may very well be chaos, hostility, and murder. But in New Orleans, at least for Nicolas Cage, there's life after death.

---

1 http://www.theculturalgutter.com/screen/synechdoche_arizona.html

The Shock Of The Stiff

When there's no more room in hell, the articles will be about zombies. So, here it is: a postmodern examination of the zombie, and a chance for me to use up all my five-dollar words. And yes, I will be quoting Baudrillard.

You've been warned.

Let's start by saying that zombies are thoroughly postmodern. The zombie is what Arthur Kroker calls the somatic body, the anti/ante-verbal part of ourselves with which we have lost contact and suppressed through our determination to posit language as the be-all and end-all of existence, through the desire to be semiotic. But the zombie is also the epitome of Kroker's panic body, which results from the breakdown of our semiotic system. Hence, the zombie attacks us from both sides, in the bodies we have left behind and the bodies we are reluctant to embrace.

George A. Romero's films in particular take place in what Kroker describes in *The Postmodern Scene* as "the violent edge between ecstasy and decay; between the melancholy lament of postmodernism over death of the grand signifiers of modernity—consciousness, truth, sex, capital, power—and the ecstatic nihilism of ultramodernism; between the body as a torture chamber and pleasure-palace…"

As *Night of the Living Dead* (1968) opens, heroine Barbra and her bother Johnny are visiting their mother's grave. Within minutes, a zombie attacks them and Johnny is killed. Mentally unhinged by the incident, Barbra flees to a nearby farmhouse where she is joined by salesman Ben, a family, and a pair of teenagers all hiding from the menace of the ghouls. The house becomes a microcosm of social stresses and forced cooperation as the group attempts (unsuccessfully) to survive until morning.

The farmhouse is precariously perched on Kroker's violent edge between ecstasy and decay; between the survivors' fierce and logical determination to live and the shambling onslaught of the zombies, who progress successfully without either ideology or meaning. The house is much like the postmodern condition as described by

101

Buadrillard: "a space radiating with power but also cracked, like a shattered windshield holding together." It hums with the energy of the nuclear family, but as nuclear father Harry Cooper observes, arguing for retreat to the basement, "There are a million windows up here. A million ways for those things to get in."

The only character that truly realizes the death of the grand signifiers is Barbra, whose constant, unanswerable question, "What's happening?" expresses the panic of the situation most aptly. Likewise, Barbra's mental and physical apathy, her total surrender to the situation turns out to be the most rational response. While the other characters fight against the encroaching darkness—boarding doors and windows, hoarding weapons and food, and attempting escape—Barbra sits motionless, waiting for the death that is slouching toward her. She is in shock: Kroker's "shock of the real" and "shock of the stiff". Because this is more than just panic; it is horror. And the only realistic response to such overwhelming horror is an evanescent desire, "the ecstatic nihilism of ultramodernism". Although this suicidal urge may seem irrational, in the context of Romero's films it can be read as a rational desire for a sense of finality.

For those fighting the zombies, what's scary is not dying at the ghouls' hands, but becoming one of them, not being able to stay dead, realizing that when death ceases to have meaning, so does life. Johnny's death leaves Barbra shattered and immobile because she has invested the concept of death with meaning. But when he returns to her as one of the zombies, she suddenly becomes active again. In the face of semiotic breakdown, she panics, and tries to escape. But the only way to escape is to beat the system—to die and stay dead. Without doubt, this is a panic response; the flight half of the fight or flight urge.

Perhaps most importantly and probably most horrifyingly, the story of Romero's films is one of aftermath, of something that has already happened, that cannot be reversed. No last minute strategy to prevent the zombies, because they are already here. This is not racing against time; it is turning on the television to find that the race ended long ago (just as the characters in the films turn on their sets to find a nation already engulfed by death). What Romero's characters experience is a sudden coming into Kroker's "fin-de-millennium consciousness which... uncovers a great arc of disintegration and decay against the background radiation of parody, kitsch, and burnout."

This is the sudden, cold sweat surety of knowledge that the end has been here for some time. The decay is laid bare as zombies parody life in all its gory, kitschy glory and burnout starts: media stop broadcasting, power goes out, and it's actually darker after the dawn.

(Especially when they let Zach Snyder direct the remake.)

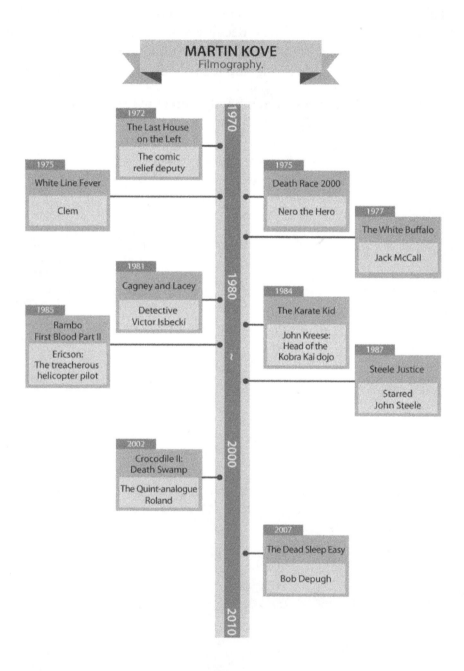

Shopping For Pants
With Martin Kove

There's a pair of pants in the bottom drawer of my dresser. They don't fit me. In fact, they're kind of ugly. They're chocolate brown with thick vertical half-hound's-tooth white stripes, a trio of faux-bone oblong buttons (non-functional) running up the side of each pocket and belt loops wide enough to accommodate a belt half a cow wide.

They're made of (I'm going to guess) cotton, although they're a little slick to the touch to make that argument convincingly, and the only label anywhere on them is a lonely "38" on the inside waist.

So if they don't fit, and I don't like the way they look, why don't I get rid of them? Well, mostly because they're not my pants. They're Martin Kove's.

If you don't immediately recognize the name, don't sweat it. A lot of people don't, even though Martin Kove has a pretty impressive filmography. He was the comic relief deputy in Wes Craven's notorious *The Last House on the Left*, the fey Nero the Hero in Paul Bartel's *Death Race 2000*, the Quint-analogue Roland in Gary Jones' *Crocodile II: Death Swamp* and starred in Robert Boris' *Steele Justice* ("You don't recruit John Steele. You unleash him."). He also appeared in such underrated classics as Jonathan Kaplan's *White Line Fever* and J. Lee Thompson's *The White Buffalo*, and had a recurring role as Detective Victor Isbecki on *Cagney and Lacey*.

But Martin is probably better known as Ericson, the treacherous helicopter pilot in George P. Cosmatos' *Rambo, First Blood Part II*, and best known as John "Sweep the leg" Kreese, head of the Kobra Kai dojo in John G. Alvidson's *The Karate Kid* (parts I - III).

I first met Martin at the American Film Market in 2005. He was there to meet with Nu Image, the producers of Sylvester Stallone's *Rambo* (2008), to see if Ericson was returning in the sequel. He wasn't.

Which, in 2007, left Martin free (or at least not expensive) to join the cast of a film I wrote called *The Dead Sleep Easy*. He joined the production team in Guadalajara in January and after moving from the hotel room we'd reserved for him to a suite at the Hilton, wanted to go shopping for wardrobe. As the writer (and one of the few members of the team who spoke a smattering of Spanish), I was deemed expendable for the day's shoot and nominated to accompany Martin on the outing.

As we wandered around open-air markets and storefronts, people started to recognize Martin. They didn't necessarily know who he was, but they knew he was somebody. Martin would smile indulgently and mention *The Karate Kid*, and peoples' faces would light up. And so, in between anecdotes about Sam Peckinpah and conversations about whether his character would wear natural or synthetic fabrics, Martin signed autographs and posed for photos with fans.

We ended up at a store called *El Charro* that specialized in traditional mariachi costumes and cowboy fashions straight out of *The Three Amigos*. The staff was instantly enamored with Martin, and he had found the look his character needed. Martin popped in and out of the change room, adding shirts and pants to a pile of desired purchases. As the stack grew I tallied in my head, and began to understand how movies go over budget.

But Martin had come equipped for the retail experience with a selection of eight by ten glossies of himself. The sales staff each got one. So did the cashier and the manager. And when the bill came due, he quietly asked if that was their best price. He talked in broad terms about what exposure in a film can do for a business, and how they might want to take that into consideration. I caught on, stepped in, and eventually negotiated a 15% discount in return for credit on the film.

Martin wore some of the clothes in the film and left others in his suite when he went back to Hollywood. I ended up with the pants.

Searching for clean clothes the other day, I ran across them, and it set me wondering, is that what celebrity comes down to? A 15% discount on pants in Guadalajara? Maybe, but I think it's something more than that. Because someone like me keeps those pants, and writes an article about them. Which someone like you then reads. Something makes them more than just pants, and I think I know what it is.

The characters Martin Kove has played are part of him now, sutured to him like Peter Pan's mischievous shadow. And whether you recognize him or not, you sense how those characters—those extra lives led— make him larger than life. At least 15% larger.

That day at *El Charro*, when the bill was paid, minus the discount, Martin took me aside and told me I should have held out for more.

Looking back on it, he was right.

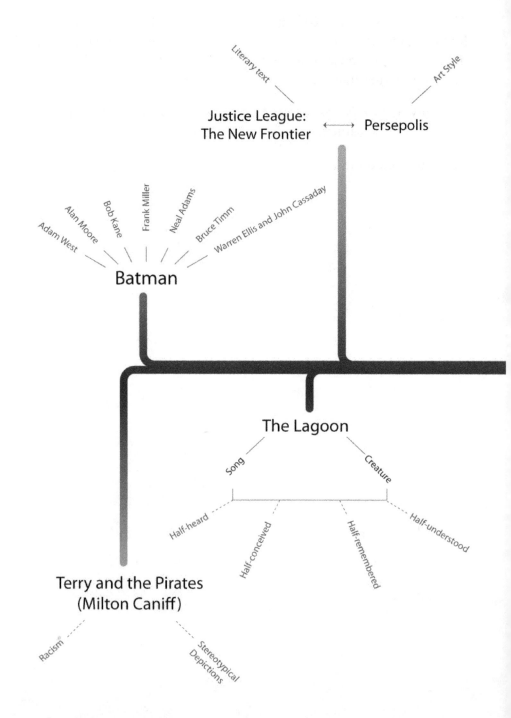

COMICS

Carol Borden

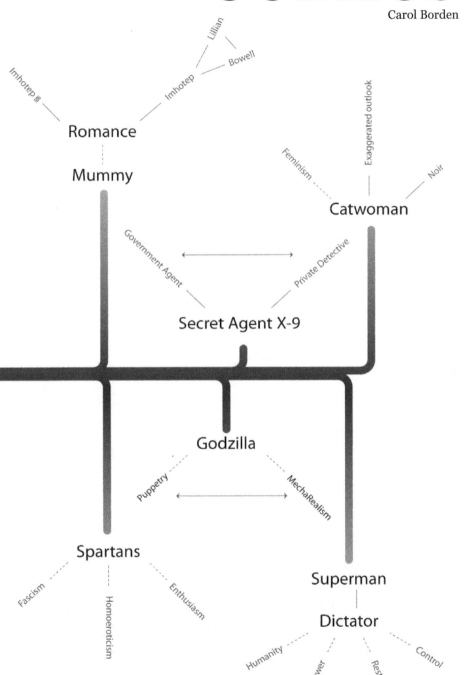

13 Ways of Looking at a Bat

Among twenty empty warehouses,
The only moving thing
Was the eye of the Batman.
—sorta Wallace Stevens[1]

You should know right from the start that I'm a terrible geek—not extremely geeky, but bad at being a geek. Continuity in the sense of an overarching, epic and harmonized chronology just isn't that important to me. What I really like about comics is the possibility of seeing different versions of the same character or even the same story. To me, comics are a mythic media using shared characters and stories.

Sure, it's still corporate and commodified and god knows artists get screwed. But there is so much possibility within a simple discipline: a boy sees his parents gunned down in an alley, swears to avenge them and grows up to be a vigilante. It's mythic, only this time with by-lines.

There's a couple of pages in writer Warren Ellis and artist John Cassaday's Planetary/Batman crossover, *Night on Earth* (Wildstorm, 2007) that I've been thinking about. Planetary is a secret organization busy uncovering the "hidden history of mankind." They claim to be "archaeologists of the impossible." In *Night on Earth*, Planetary are in Gotham City busy tracking down a kid who unfortunately causes reality to shift all around him like he's flipping channels. Gotham slips from one possibility to another and because it's Gotham, Batman gets involved and moves through several incarnations himself from Bob Kane's to Adam West's to Frank Miller's and each one is slightly—or radically—different from the others. And it all happens in the alley where Bruce Wayne saw his parents gunned down.

Those few pages really struck me. They made me think of all the different Batmans: detective Batman, ninja Batman, crotchety right wing vigilante Batman, monomaniacal Batman, Batman with baggage, trapped in a well Batman, campy Batman, deputized peace officer Batman, science Batman, loner Batman, Batman leading his own flock of superheros, future Batman, the sorta Peter Parker Batman on *The Batman* cartoon, Batman created by crime and creating criminals.

And while for the purposes of this essay it doesn't matter which ones I like and which ones I don't that doesn't mean I don't have preferences. My feelings about Adam West in the Batman tv show have been inconstant. As a kid, I took every peril very seriously ("Oh, no, Batman is going to be turned into a giant key!"). When I was older, that Batman was painfully uncool. Now I love camp. *Superfriends* Batman left me cold. His reliance on gadgets, his lack of superpowers and his relentless toadying for the Man just irritate me. Both these shows might well also be responsible for my abiding Robin issues. While clearly seminal and definitely testosterrific, Frank Miller's ninja Batman is starting to wear on me. I am ever fond of Bob Kane's stiff and pointy-eared 1940s Batman.

The stripped down, streamlined Batman from Bruce Timm's *Batman: The Animated Series* and *Batman Adventures* is the Batman in my heart and I don't care who knows it. For me, somehow, that Batman embodies what Jules Feiffer says in *The Great Comic Book Heroes*: "With Superman we won; with Batman we held our own."[2] That Batman's victories are often about holding his own, in surviving. He is vulnerable without being entirely defined by that vulnerability—a phobic boy trapped in a well—or a fascist, psychotic thug or a schizoid mirror image of the Joker. Although, the Joker thing is still interesting

So with, say, *Batman Begins*, I can think it's very good and very interesting even though I wouldn't make the same choices. My Bruce Wayne wasn't a boy trapped in a well. I like a Batman who likes bats. But the story works well, and while I might regret it's becoming canonical, I can turn to another I prefer—even one that's not as good.

Or I can wait for a new take. No one storyline ever wins for long. There's always an artist fascinated by some new take or another artist who remembers something they liked and revamps it when they get a title.

I hear that just as crows come in a murder and ravens come in an unkindness, bats come in a cloud. I can live with a cloud of Batmans floating like electrons in indeterminate relation to one another— some of them even generated in an attempt to clean up the continuity or re-appearing when an artist or writer misses an old storyline or incarnation. But if all those Batmans didn't exist in their infinite possibility, there would never be those huge multi-comic spanning arcs trying to harmonize the back story once again. And other fans wouldn't get the chance to see their favorite old Batman rise again.

One Batman doesn't supplant another. Adam West doesn't nullify Alan Moore. From Bob Kane to Frank Miller to Neal Adams to Bruce Timm to Warren Ellis and John Cassaday's, all the Batmans stand in a line holding hands. All Batmans equally.

1 Stevens, Wallace. "Thirteen Ways of Looking at a Blackbird." Eds. Richard Ellman and Robert O'Clair. The Norton Anthology of Modern Poetry: Second Edition. New York: W. W. Norton & Company, 1988 :287. Print.
2 Feiffer, Jules. The Great Comic Book Heroes. New York: Bonanza Books, 1965: 27. Print.

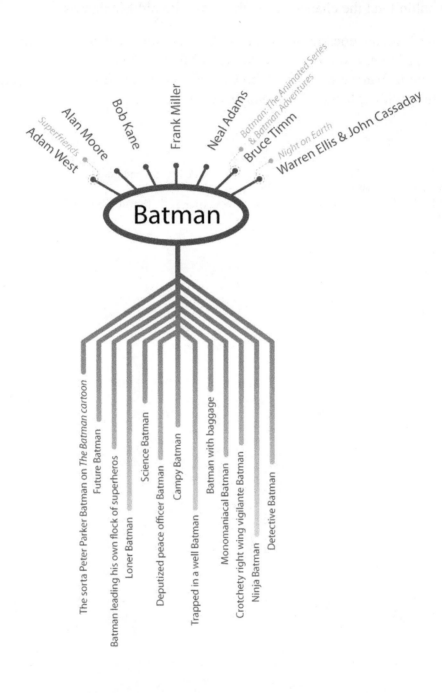

Space to Move

The same week that I walked over to the rep theater to see *Persepolis*. I watched the straight-to-DVD *Justice League: The New Frontier*. And, yes, it's probably wrong to write about *The New Frontier* within pixels of *Persepolis*, even if they're both comics that became animated movies with very different results.

I admit it. I like *Persepolis* better as a movie than as a book. Marjane Satrapi and Vincent Paronnaud fuse Satrapi's two volume comic memoir about her life in post-revolutionary Tehran and European exile into one movie. The story seems smoother. But the real difference for me is the art. The film gives it some space.

While she doesn't paint with a single kitten hair, Satrapi's work gestures toward Persian miniatures, even sharing their geometric focus. But Pantheon's 9" x 6" book seems less like a collection of miniatures than cramped Victorian curating, with panels squished closely together without much border. Even a miniature needs space. On screen, her art has more depth and texture, from rough pastel shading and gray washes to tumbling flowers and twining branches. The blacks are much more expansive.

And Satrapi uses the movie to explore different styles for each narrative, from a blackened out Social Realist woodcut look for the Iran-Iraq War to the overarching frame of Marjane at the airport, the only segment in color. Her Uncle Anoush's story begins as an animated miniature before sliding seamlessly into a puppet play of his flight to the Soviet Union. My favorite segment depicts the tempting of Reza Khan to become shah. I love its mockery of the British diplomat (Edmond Ironside?) and Reza Khan's self-importance and vanity. Their flapping arms are perfect.

But her story also escapes the reverence in which we might hold it. The respectable ratios. The dominance of text over art. The binding that makes it harder for the art to open up like the jasmine spilling down the screen. Pantheon has nice graphic novels, but there's an ambivalence in the materials themselves, an unwillingness to risk not being taken seriously as books, even when some of the conventions of comics publishing—the ratios, the binding, the borders, the paper— might serve Satrapi's art better.

Still what can compare with the luminosity and absolute blackness of the film? The monochromatic silence so much deeper than the book? How do I go back to static Satrapi when she's created something perfect with Vincent Paronnaud?

More brightly-colored than *Persepolis* but darker-toned than Warner Bros.' *Justice League* tv series, *The New Frontier* is set before the Justice League became the Justice League. The story addresses the Cold War, McCarthyism and the threat within using heroes in capes, tights and star-spangled shorts. In their 90 minutes, Darwyn Cooke and Bruce Timm make a nice allegory for contemporary America, focusing on the heroes' relationships, the capture of the Martian J'onn J'onzz, and rampant paranoia. But the end's rushed. There's a monster kinda out of nowhere. Superman suddenly stands up for what's right and calls everyone to look past a feared alien threat— whether pinko or green—and work together. It's a nice little trick, an homage to 1950s alien menace movies that are anti-Communist or anti-McCarthyite depending on how you squint.

Better fans than I can write about the truncated story and the references to DC comics history. Really, I'm not the one you want to go to for that. I can say that Cooke's art had more space and flexibility before it was animated straight to DVD. I didn't expect the movie to compete with the books' expressive art or multiple artistic styles; and it doesn't. But while the film's slicker, it's not as painful as Disney Hellboy. J'onn J'onzz remains tragically expressive. Blocky Korean War Wonder Woman is an Amazon's Amazon and who doesn't like to see pointy-eared Batman wearing purple gloves? But while superhero cartoons—and maybe cartoons in general—benefit from *The New Frontier*'s new medium, I can't say that *The New Frontier* does. Its sacrifice is certainly appreciated, but Cooke's art flattens out on the screen.

It's funny that the more literary text would benefit so much more from its transposition. *The New Frontier* becomes more stereotypical on screen, while *Persepolis* escapes the pieties of literature with all the force of a francophone woman singing, "Eye of the Tiger." Literature is supposed to be more expansive than genre. Superheros are supposed to be tough.

But there are little overlaps. Both movies are about profoundly distrustful societies turning against themselves to battle their own fear. Satrapi humanizes what is too easily understood as dehumanized political history, seeking solidarity in our common humanity. *The New Frontier* presents the parable of a Martian squatting in a black site cell. One is a helluva lot more respectable than the other, but learning to love the alien is always worthwhile.

Weighing the Hearts of the Dead

In this age of fast zombies and vampires sparkling in the sun, maybe it's time to remember the overlooked, the eternally cursed, the bandaged, leathery and passionate undead: mummies.

Mummies are all about undying love. Not only does the resurrected Imhotep doesn't only try to bring his dead love back to life in the 1999 film *The Mummy*, he does the same in the 1930s film after meeting Helen, the very image of his beloved Anck-es-en-Amon. In the graphic novel, *The Professor's Daughter*, Imhotep falls in love with Lillian, a woman who resembles his dead love, lost two thousand years ago. Maybe that's why Maat weighs hearts in *The Book of the Dead.*

Written by Joann Sfar and drawn by Emmanuel Guibert, *The Professor's Daughter* was first published in France in 1997 and has been translated into English by Alexis Siegel for First Second Books' 2007 edition. Guibert is now best known for *The Photographer* and *Alan's War: The Memories of G.I. Alan Cope*, books about the experience of war. Sfar is probably best known for *Dungeon*, his Dungeons and Dragons parody collaboration with Lewis Trondheim. Sfar and Guibert collaborate on another children's series—one about space pirates—*Sardine in Outer Space*, with art by Sfar and a script by Guibert. But *The Professor's Daughter* is my favorite of all my collaborations. The London they have created is an idealized Victorian one: whiskers and tweed, professors and antiquarians, Scotland Yard and Queen Victoria, poisoning and propriety. I wish Guibert would illustrate more of Sfar's stories. It's nice to see his ink in the service of fun.

Guibert's art is lovely, the ephemeral graphite, deep inks and shading ground the book in three dimensions. The colors and lines give it a nice Late Victorian feel. The hand-rendered serif lettering on the cover is delicately antique. Sfar's script is charming and filled with derring-do—murder, close escapes, dockside gangs, courtroom drama and kidnapping. The book's also funny:

> Imhotep [aiming a gun at Professor Bowell]: I love Lillian
> and we're going to get married.
> Bowell: You are the property of the British Museum. You are
> dead. Stay out of this!
> Lillian [in Imhotep's arms]: Imhotep, where are you taking
> me?
> Imhotep: To Cairo![1]

Sfar and Guibert's Imhotep is not *The Mummy*'s vengeful and desperately lonely high priest. This is Imhotep IV, Prince of Egypt, and, as indicated in the passage above, he has a problem. He's a mummy in the Victorian era, and despite the fact that he dresses, walks, talks, drinks tea and smokes like a gentleman, he is legally not human. He is an antiquity and property of the British Museum. The man who discovered him, Professor Bowell, is content to have Imhotep displayed in a glass case forever.

The professor's daughter, Lillian, awakens Imhotep to accompany her on a walk in Kensington Gardens and Imhotep falls in love with her, but unlike other mummies, other Imhoteps, he does not try to channel his beloved's soul into Lillian's body. He wants to marry her. Lillian fears that Imhotep only loves her for her resemblance to an ancient dead woman and "want[s] no part of his neurosis."[2] But Imhotep IV is also wanted for murder by Scotland Yard, which seizes all the mummies in London for examination as suspects before finally arresting a very much unmummified Lillian as a murderess. So it comes down to romantic angst with linen wrappings, grilled crickets and the examining of hearts.

And I don't mean to spoil anything, but Imhotep's father, Imhotep III, also falls in love too easily. Is it because he's a mummy or because he's named, "Imhotep?" Imhotep III's approach to love—kidnapping—is just as supervillainous as his approach to fatherhood. Imhotep III wants to make right a marriage he prevented 2000 years ago, while saving his son from the Queen's justice and will do so by any means necessary, including forcing Queen Victoria to marry him. Prof. Bowell, on the other hand, is an aloof and preoccupied scientist, apparently a good man—and an adventurous hero in Sfar's later stories—but not an attentive, affectionate father.

While vampires are all hunger and desire and no one wants to think about the love lives of zombies, love weighs heavily on the hearts of mummies—or at least mummies named, "Imhotep." Incidentally, there was a historical Imhotep, but he wasn't a pharaoh. He was: "Chancellor of the King of Egypt, Doctor, First in line after the King of Upper Egypt, Administrator of the Great Palace, Hereditary nobleman, High Priest of Heliopolis, Builder, Chief Carpenter, Chief Sculptor and Maker of Vases in Chief."[3]

He was an architect, physician and later a god. But as far as I know, the historical Imhotep never attempted to reincarnate his ancient love in another woman's body or traveled across time to escort his sweetheart to the bandstand in Queen Victoria's Kensington Gardens.

1 Sfar, Joann and Emmanuel Guibert. The Professor's Daughter. Trans. Alexis Siegel.
New York: First Second Books, 2007: 20. Print.
2 Sfar and Guibert 35
3 "Imhotep." Wikipedia.org. Wikipedia, n.d. Web. Oct. 2009.
<http://en.wikipedia.org/wiki/Imhotep>

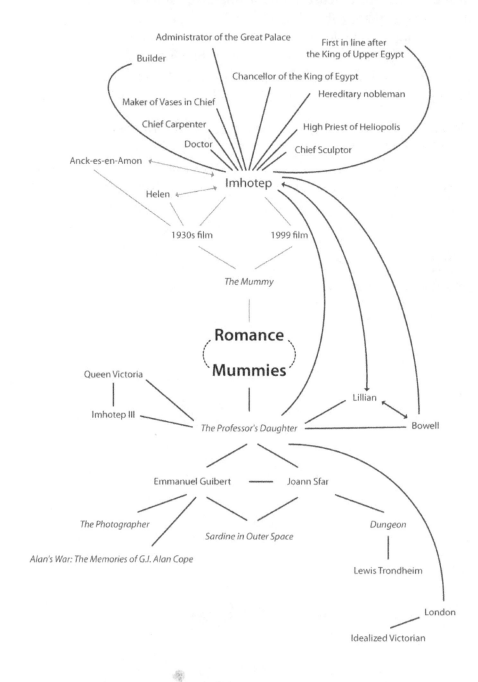

Catwoman: Silicon-Injected

In 2001, *Catwoman* was everything I ever wanted in a comic. I admit I was a sucker for her new look. A woman's stompy black boots are her pride and Catwoman's boots were stompy, black and flat after years of thigh high Pretty Woman stilettos. Not to mention that zippers with rings, black leather, kitty ears and experimental night vision goggles are just cool, way cooler than purple latex. The art by Darwyn Cooke, Cameron Stewart and Mike Allred was loose, expressive and playful. Ed Brubaker's writing was hardboiled, but took after Raymond Chandler's fragile and battered humanism rather than Dashiell Hammett's breezy amorality.

As in Chandler, Selina Kyle (aka Catwoman) discovers that getting ahead as a hero is often just being able to walk away and call it even and that a second chance is its own reward. A lot of beat up Robert Mitchum look-alikes teach her about regret, loss and the necessity of doing the right thing—from offering a petty thief the second chance his father never had to giving a diner waitress $100,000 for years of tolerating the "Midwest Mob." I am a total sucker for all that— nice art, good writing, noir, the vulnerability in standing up for what's right. It was too good to last.

While I was busy enjoying the writing (old guys filled with regret, lesbian punklings in love) and the art (so fun and expressive), I should have paid more attention to the letters column because, in the end, I am not the demographic DC wants. Fans complained that the art was cartoony and when Darwyn Cooke and Cameron Stewart moved on, Catwoman's costume underwent another redesign. The new costume wasn't a purple bodysuit but hearkened back to Frank Miller's "realistic" re-imagining of Selina Kyle as a dominatrix. The next thing I knew Brubaker was still writing, but Catwoman had a new pair of boots—low pointy heel, but ankle-breaking just the same—and a larger pair of breasts, which have been steadily expanding since.

Writing and art are carefully balanced in comics and I honestly couldn't say which weighs more heavily in my decision to pass over a comic or not. At least I couldn't until Catwoman. I might have felt it in some way before, as I cringed through copies of X-Men, but now I know that the deal breaker for me is breasts. Superhero boobs pretty much represent everything I find painful and alienating in comics. Teen heroes and sidekicks have breasts the size of real adult women. Full grown superheroes have breasts that are impossibly huge, impossibly perky and impossible to subvert no matter how artists try. They endure as buffed, waxed and gleaming as a vintage Sunbird and, along with every superhero's musculature, as carefully highlighted in white cg airbrush fuzz as conversion van fantasy art. Yes, the hot art in comics right now looks a little automotive to me. If only they used larger metal flake and more chrome on their rides.

Fans complained that the art was cartoony and unrealistic. I think what they meant was that rendered in a more obviously abstracted way, wearing a more practical (in the same sense that Batman's costume is practical) outfit, Catwoman wasn't special private time material anymore. The lesbianism Catwoman's usual fans want isn't cute girls in love, it's a little more Reform School Girls. And the outfits they want Catwoman to wear aren't for crimefighting, or even catburglery. Batman's life in leather might be a subtext, but Catwoman's life in latex isn't. Her old costume features her breasts in a way that rendering her nude cannot: shiny, sleek and frequently nipple-less. Somehow, the absence of nipples makes Catwoman appear more naked than naked.

Before Brubaker's run, the writing was frequently all about putting Catwoman into certain places, positions and purple latex. It reminds me of porn narratives. I'm not denigrating porn here. It's just that porn narratives are not character or story driven. They are goal-oriented. They provide short hand reasons for why things happen in the story: Protagonists meet because he's a pizza delivery guy or she's stealing a statue of Bast.

So on one side, it's me (hi!), all excited about Catwoman in her 'kickers, finally noir like I always wanted. On the other side, there are many, many more male fans with particular needs they expect Catwoman will fulfill. I think on both sides we look at comic breasts in the same way, take them as the same signs, and draw different conclusions. Every time I see the huge, buffed and sanded, silicon-injected, all-weather rated breasts of superheroines, I see all the desire and expectation and hope that fans can put into them and all the impossibility of those breasts in the world (or maybe even their terrifying reality). I see a reminder that Catwoman is intended for another audience. But even though it seemed there's no way to compromise between my cool antihero and their safe fetish pin-up, something broke through. For 25 issues, I got mine.

Stainless

Recently, one of my friends told me that Superman was an inch from becoming a dictator. It didn't seem likely to me, but I didn't have any arguments, just a sense that Superman wasn't inclined toward world domination. Luckily enough, the public library system provided me with, *The Man from Krypton: A Closer Look at Superman*, a 2006 collection of essays edited by Glenn Yeffeth.

The Man from Krypton is part of Benbella Books Smart Pop series. Smart Pop includes geekily academic and academically geeky books on *The Matrix*, *NYPD Blue*, King Kong, *The Golden Compass*, *Farscape*, *Pride and Prejudice* and anything Joss Whedon. Sadly, aside from the pastel Lichtensteinish cover, there are no pictures. Still, it's a fun book with essays on Krypton, Christopher Reeve, *Smallville*, Lois and that one by Larry Niven about how Superman'd kill Lois if they had sex. Ladies, I suggest staying away from it. Gruesome. *The Man from Krypton* also gave me some perspective on how the Superman might differ from other Men of Steel, say Josef Stalin (despite obvious differences like never creating a system of gulags, Phantom Zone aside).

Sure, Superman has the ability to set himself up as King of the World, but he chooses not to. That choice counts, just as my own choices not to be an asshole count. I think I hadn't read much Superman because it was hard for me to sympathize with him—his power, his belief in Truth, Justice and the American Way. Maybe as I get older and more aware of how I can hurt people, I sympathize more with Clark, who can hurt people every day if he's not careful all the time.

In "History of Violence," David Hopkins surveys hundreds of covers and consults an uber Superman geek friend. He discovers that Superman damages a lot of property, but not people. He concludes that Superman's nature is "one of power, restraint and, finally, theatrics."[1] It's a side issue, but theatrics is worth pondering. Jules Feiffer wrote in another book that Clark Kent was Superman's cover and reflected his view of humanity[2]. Hopkins adds, "Clark Kent, the mild-mannered

Daily Planet reporter, is an act, but, to some degree, so is Superman. Both hold back. Power and violence do not show the true strength and courage of a person, but control and restraint do."[3]

Screw the flying, super strength and heat vision, Superman's greatest power might well be that he's always in control. He restrains himself while appearing to hit a thug as hard as he can. But Superman never does. That restraint is exactly where stories of alternate universe or Kryptonite-addled Superman gone wrong or Superman letting loose get their thrill. The Warner Bros. animated series managed to reflect the fearsome nature of his power, mostly in the amount of crater-causing damage he took because he could and, occasionally, in his letting go on superpowerful villains like life-hating alien dictator and bad father, Darkseid. In one episode of *Justice League*, an other dimensional Superman imposes order and security by killing Lex Luthor and lobotomizing antisocial elements. Encountering this alternate self reminds Superman of what he could become and clarifies why Superman binds himself with human-imposed limits like the law and Clark's daily life. The fact that it's Superman binding himself—choosing not to be a dictator—and nothing else, is part of what worries people, mostly fictional people but also fans like my friend.

Of course, people don't just worry about what Superman could do. They worry about what Superman doesn't do. Paul Levinson agonizes over the implications of Superman's restraint in "Superman, Patriotism and Doing the Ultimate Good: Why the Man of Steel Did So Little to Stop Hitler." And what Superman doesn't do is stop World War II. Levinson's caught like a coat in a car door on why Superman lets bad things happen to good people. In his desire to maintain his suspension of disbelief, he disregards his best answer: Superman couldn't end World War II because readers in the 1940s would find it unbelievable. For Levinson, finding an explanation outside the story kills the magic. He wants to believe in Superman. And so he tugs away, pained by Superman's refusal to do more about suffering in the real world, pained by Superman's refusal to take the control people want to give him to end evil.

Levinson might not be the only one frustrated. Superman just doesn't make the world, even a comic book world, a better place, despite the universal experience of fucking things up when we're trying to make them better. Sometimes that frustration leads to dismissive representations of Superman as a boy scout or a government flunky— someone who submits to imperfect authority even though he seems to know innately what is right and good. Superman could be a tyrant for truth, justice and the American way, but he's just not that Man of Steel.

1 Hopkins, David. "History of Violence." The Man from Krypton: A Closer Look at Superman. Ed. Glenn Yeffeth. Dallas: Benbella Books, 2006: 19. Print.
2 Feiffer, Jules. The Great Comic Book Heroes. New York: Bonanza Books, 1965: 19. Print.
3 Hopkins 19.

Frank Miller's Hot Gates

A feeling's been gnawing deep inside me for a while. A feeling that maybe Frank Miller's hypermasculine antiheros and faceless, breast-thrusting women are exactly what they seem, not just sketchy parody. After reading *300*, Miller's 1998 account of the Spartans at Thermopylae, I don't have any doubt: Miller means it. His aesthetic is fascist.

Fascism isn't all jackboots and *Ilsa, She-Wolf of the SS*. Sometimes it's well-hung Spartans toting big spears. In this case, *300* is beautiful with art worthy of a picture book. Lynn Varley's goauche-like washes and thick spatters of rain, blood and ash are lovely. Some panels look like ukiyo-e woodcuts, and Miller demonstrates a fluid line reminiscent of Will Eisner. In prose worthy of Thea von Harbou, Miller sings of 300 Spartans' defense of "Reason," "Justice" and "Law" against "darkness," "mysticism" and the "stupid" ways of the past:

> *One hundred* nations descend upon us. Snorting, snarling desert *beasts*. Howling *barbarians*. The armies of all Asia--pledged to *crush* the impertinent republics of Greece—to make *slaves* of the only *Free Men* the world has ever *known* (all emphases Miller's).

It is beautiful work and pernicious as hell. Yukio Mishima would love this picture book. I'm not sure that would trouble Frank Miller at all. He's probably spent too much time with *Sun and Steel*.[1]

Fascist aesthetics don't only celebrate authoritarianism. They also focus on ideal leaders; the exercise of will over the body and the masses; ecstatic self-abnegation and self-surrender; freedom from weakness; physical perfection; death as transcendence and death as ultimate victory. In her essay, "Fascinating Fascism," Susan Sontag writes that fascist aesthetics "endorse two seemingly opposite states, egomania and servitude."[2]

And then there is sexuality. Miller keeps bringing homosexuality up and then dismissing it—like someone else brought it up. I sure didn't. It's not like sex is necessary in a war story and nothing's more irritating than Freud when he's right, but this whole comic is tumescent. And I'm not sure it's even fair to call the sexuality repressed, what with naked Spartans sleeping spears between their legs and those spears later erupting from the mouths of Persian scouts. And Thermopylae's English translation, "The Hot Gates," becomes positively turgid, as if the Spartans were dead sperm blocking the Persians' entrance into Greece "herself," or something more man-sex, given Delios the storyteller's focus on butts.

But the homoeroticism is denied and the Spartans presented, historical sources be damned, not only as not homosexual but as homophobes, spitting insults at "pretty" Athenian "boy-lovers" in an attempt to provide a different context for lines like, "I'm ready for my punishment, Sir." The threat gay men pose is no different than the threat women pose. Sexuality and sentiment are weakness. Miller's ideal manly, manly Spartans aren't weak.

The narrator of *300* reports:
> 'Goodbye, my love,' [Leonidas] doesn't say it. There is no room for softness. Not in Sparta. No place for weakness.
> Only the *hard* and *strong* may call themselves Spartans.
> Only the *hard*.
> Only the *strong*.

Just so everyone understands that Leonidas totally could get some but being so virile, he's not interested, his wife remarks that his plan to die at Thermopylae explains his "enthusiasm" the night before. Leonidas responds, "Sparta needs sons." At least Miller drew her with a face.

In *300*, it's not just homosexuality or women that are filthy and degrading. Sex and love are tainted in themselves. Manliness is killing and dying, no kissing. Sontag writes:

> [S]exuality [is] converted into the magnetism of leaders
> and the joy of followers. The fascist ideal is to transform
> sexual energy into a "spiritual" force, for the benefit of the
> community. The erotic… is always present as a temptation,
> with the most admirable response being a heroic repression
> of the sexual impulse.

And we are treated to the magnetism of leaders and the joy of followers. "Joined—fused—a single creature—indivisible, impenetrable, unstoppable—we push."

132

300 is the first time I've ever read something written in first person plural omniscient. The style reads so well I didn't notice until, halfway through, I started thinking about fascism. It leads the reader to identify with the Spartans' identification with Leonidas. "We" narrate the story as Spartans who—unlike Xerxes' "enslaved" army—chose to lose ourselves in the phalanx, in destroying Asian hordes and in Leonidas, the singular hero who makes us all heroic. How is this freedom? Like Sontag says it is all "egomania and servitude."

In the end, fascist aesthetics celebrate the ecstatic and transcendent purity of death. In *300*, the Spartan goal is death and that goal is fulfilled in the last chapter, "Victory." Miller focuses not just on death itself, but on mortification of the flesh. Leonidas has more in common with Mel Gibson's pizzafied Jesus than Yukio Mishima's Saint Sebastian or von Harbou's static Siegfried pieta. Leonidas' mortification is victory--not holding off the Persians until the Athenian navy arrives, not even killing Xerxes, in all his pierced, effeminate, dark-skinned glory. Stelios, the sidekick youth, finally becomes a man and Spartan by dying. Death itself is victory.

1 Mishima, Yukio. Sun and Steel. New York: Kodansha International, 2003. Print.
2 Sontag, Susan. "Fascinating Fascism." New York Review of Books. February 6, 1975.
Marcuse, Harold. The Holocaust: Interdisciplinary Perspectives. UC Santa Barbara, Mar. 2006. Web. Feb. 2007

Tired of Saving You

There's a panel in *Secret Agent X-9* that fascinates me. In it, X-9 tells a woman and her father, "I'm tired of saving your lives." The panel appears in the second half of Dashiell Hammett's first Secret Agent X-9 storyline, "You're the Top!" That's right—Dashiell Hammett scripted a daily comic. And he did it with Alex Raymond, whose *Flash Gordon* was launched the same month, drew all seven storylines collected in Kitchen Sink Press' 1990 *Secret Agent X-9*. King Features Syndicate made a pretty good match with Hammett and Raymond, too bad they couldn't leave them be.

According to Bill Blackbeard's introduction, there was some conflict around who exactly X-9 was. King Features wanted a government agent and Hammett wanted a private detective more in line with his work as an author and former Pinkerton. Hammett tried to compromise with a secret agent whose cover was as a private detective, possibly following the plot of a 1933 William Powell film, *Private Detective 62*, about a G-man who retires and becomes an private investigator. But to get what they wanted, the people at King were willing to alter Hammett's scripts before handing them off to Raymond. This created strange continuity and straight out consistency problems around X-9's nebulous identity. "You can call me Dexter—it's not my name, but it'll do," X-9 says. Is he a private eye? A secret agent? A G-man? What agency is he working for? Why is he paid by the people he saves?

What was King Features thinking when they decided to shift a writer they'd hired for his hardboiled cred over to writing the story of a government agent? Seems like a waste to me, but how many syndicates are happy to let people do their thing? Suffice it to say that of the four storylines with Hammett's byline, two were certainly fully scripted by him: "You're the Top" and "The Mystery of the Silent Guns." His contract was up halfway through the third, "The Martyn Case." *The Saint* author Leslie Charteris took over after Hammett quit. Charteris left a few months later and stories were thereafter attributed to "Robert Stone"—a house name similar to Alan Smithee in film but without the judgment. Blackbeard details the history much better than I ever could.

"The Martyn Case" is kind of obnoxious what with its reliance on blatant bathos—a widowed mother, a wealthy aunt, a kidnapped ingénue and the newsy who loves her. It's saccharine enough to make me feel sick deep down inside. I have a hard time with ineffective damsels and sidekick kids. I think all that hackneyed peril and sugarless bathos is more the fault of King's softboiled house writers than Hammett, who casually describes Sam Spade as a "blond Satan" in *The Maltese Falcon*. Ironic detachment is rarely broken by anything other than exhaustion in Hammett's writing.

The remaining two Hammett storylines are engaging in different ways. "The Mystery of the Silent Guns" is old timey serial fun with a masked gangster and his radio set up in a secret cavern lair. Not to mention that the Mask is allied with nefarious cowboys. I always like the villains in old serials that wear hoods or robes and might have an electro-magnetic ray, but rely on the traditional methods of organized crime. They're like supervillains in the awkward tween years— almost Magneto, but no mutant powers and toting tommyguns, but too magenta for Al Capone's pin stripe set.

"You're the Top" is the best storyline of Hammett's run. And that brings me back to exhaustion and the panel I mentioned. Halfway through, "You're the Top," a ragged and bandaged X-9 tells Evelyn he's tired of rescuing her father and her. He has every reason to be as they chase her crazed father through the city, trying to save him from the Top and themselves from dad's panicked attempt to burn them alive. But in a way, that panel and that statement are the last things I expect. The 1934 image of a roughed up X-9 is more visceral to me than later attempts to achieve the same effect—a bloodied Superman or haggard Bruce Willis flicking his tongue at his cut lip. X-9 doesn't awe with his ability to take damage. It is his fragility that is arresting. Raymond's brushwork shows a man worn down and ready to drop but needing to do a little more. The sequences that follow—X-9 steadying himself against a wall and later collapsing in a policeman's arms in the last panel—are powerful. His statement becomes more a bone weary truth than a superhero's resentment or an anti-hero's preference for acting alone.

I can't help wondering about the parallels between X-9 and Hammett at that same moment. Hammett euphorically racing through his first comic story, hoping King will help him, pushing his work and his new medium, weary and not necessarily saving anything in the end, but trying just the same.

Yellow Peril

I've learned something reading *Terry and the Pirates:* There's no way around the yellow peril in the Golden Age. Good comics sometimes have racist renderings in them.

IDW Publishing's Library of American Comics is reprinting Milton Caniff's 1934-1946 *Terry and the Pirates* with archival material and even a nice ribbon bookmark. The strip features boy adventurer Terry Lee and manly journalist Pat Ryan's journey through China. The Sunday strips are in color. The books' ratios recall a time when newspapers' daily strips were higher quality than comic books. In volume 2, Pat is kinda wooden and Terry's wide-eyed surprise and sweater are creepy sidekick. But, as Jules Feiffer notes in *The Great Comic Book Heroes*: "Who cared about [heroes], when there were oriental villains around?"[1]

Enter the Dragon Lady, stereotypically duplicitous and ruthless but also a pirate captain and, later, a nationalist leader. She has an anti-hero frisson. Terry and Pat's guide Connie, though, is an embarrassing stereotype, buckteeth, dialect and all. In another setting, I might think that Connie was a different species, the only one of his kind. No other Chinese character looks like him; very few say things like, "Little missy get bump on noodle in big boom-bust."[2]

Still, Caniff researched his work meticulously. He had Chinese-American fans and informants. He wrote sympathetically about people struggling with British and French colonialism as well as the Chinese resisting the Greater East Asia Co-Prosperity Sphere. In volume 2, just months after the Rape of Nanking, the Dragon Lady gives a 4-strip speech exhorting an overthrown warlord's followers to join her in fighting the Japanese.[3] Caniff's views annoyed 2 of his publishers who were prominent isolationists. *New York Daily News'* Joe Patterson told Caniff not to write about the war in China. In response, Caniff's scripts began using "the invader" instead of, "Japanese."[4]

But as Caniff depicted the Second Sino-Japanese War, World War II revived the oriental villain. Only this time, the oriental villain was Japanese:

> Until the war we always assumed he was Chinese. But now we knew what he was! .... He often sported fanged bicuspids and drooled a lot more than seemed necessary. (If you find the image hard to imagine I refer you to his more recent incarnation in magazines like Dell's *Jungle War Stories* where it turns out he wasn't Japanese at all: He was North Vietnamese. At the time of this book's publication the wheel will, no doubt, have turned full circle and he'll be back to Chinese).[5]

I've heard the arguments about these stereotypical depictions—they are of their time, they're comedic and shouldn't be taken seriously. But from Connie to Jar-Jar Binks, what denigrates humanity more than comic relief?[6] It's easy to say that readers should overlook Connie's rendering as the conventions of a more racist time or because of Caniff's groundbreaking work chronicling and humanizing the turmoil in China. It's just as easy to dismiss the whole strip as racist while we progress on our upward trajectory, rocketing into the future. But one doesn't cancel out the other. They exist side by side.

What's striking about comics like Caniff's is not just the historical curiosity of the stereotypical depictions. It's the ways those depictions could exist now. And it's the way that right now we are doing something that people will find as painful as Connie, and we just don't know what it is.

Grant Morrison's recent DC Asian superteams skirt the edges. I like Morrison, so I'm not condemning his work, but Mother of Champions is painful. A member of Chinese superteam The Great Ten, Mother of Champions' passive, squickening power—one that's more a curse than anything the X-men agonize over—is birthing 25 supersoldiers every three days. A Chinese woman whose power is breeding for the state? It could be a criticism of the Chinese government, but it's not well-grounded enough to be. Besides, reproduction is used so often to freak out fanboys that any insect mother depiction, let alone of a

Chinese woman, is sketchy. Mother of Champions apparently picks her donors. Maybe it's an attempt to give her some agency. Still, I wonder if she decapitates them when she's done?

Meanwhile, manga fans dislike Morrison's Japanese superheros for DC's hero-culling event, *Final Crisis*.[7] They're troubled by the depiction of Japanese men as shallow fashionistas and superhero names like, "Most Excellent Superbat" and "Shy Crazy Lolita Canary" that are more like an idea of Japanese in translation than Japanese in translation—or even "engrish." Worse yet, the names come across as a gesture towards speech like Connie's, a gesture I don't think Morrison intends.

That said, Caniff's drawing of Connie is much more offensive than any of Morrison's designs. Morrison's superteams don't have buckteeth or "skin the color of ripe lemons."[8] But Caniff's work is also more grounded in the reality of the people and places he's depicting. So what do we do with that? Or the fact that Connie's comic relief and the old slanty-eyed, long-fingernailed yellow peril might distract us from recognizing perilous depictions here in comics' postmodern age?

1 Feiffer, Jules. The Great Comic Book Heroes. New York: Bonanza Books, 1965. 16. Print.
2 Caniff, Milton. The Complete Terry and the Pirates: Vol. 2: 1937-8. Ed. Dean Mullaney. San Diego: IDW Publishing, 2008. 234. Print.
3 Caniff. 226-7.
4 Caniff. 26.
5 Feiffer. 47-8.
6 To be fair, Connie has more redeeming characteristics than Jar-Jar Binks.
7 See Nenena. "Most Excellent Super What?" Paper Moon. Nenena.livejournal.com. 15 May 2008. Web. 2 Jun. 2008. <http://nenena.livejournal.com/147975.html>; and the Sooz. "Morrison, What the Hell?!" Furikku. Furikku.livejournal.com. 27 May 2008. Web. 2 Jun. 2008. <http://furikku.livejournal.com/512987.html>
8 Feiffer. 16.

Godzilla vs. MechaRealism

A while ago I watched some Godzilla movies with some people who don't exactly appreciate the aesthetics of suitmation / kigurumi, or, in less technical language, a guy in a rubber suit. One of the things I like best about Godzilla movies is that as soon as I glimpse Godzilla rising from the depths or appearing behind the mountains, I'm forced to suspend my disbelief.

I'm pretty sure it's the rubber suit and that suit serves as a reminder that realism might be ascendant, but is still only an aesthetic and not suited to every genre.

I willingly admit that there are downsides to monsters played by guys in suits, but not the one my friends assert—rubber suits are "unrealistic." I guess that means, "A giant city-devastating monster would not look like that." My personal problems with rubber suits are encompassed by one monster: Minilla, Godzilla's son. I don't know how bad Minilla is in Japanese, but in English he is unbearable. With his googly eyes, hyucking laugh and hokey Davey and Goliath voice, Minilla was made to be dubbed. His anxious jiggling is the precursor to the frenetic wigglings of monsters in live action Japanese superhero shows like *Ultraman*, *Kamen Rider* and *Mighty Morphin' Power Rangers*. Minilla was invented at a time when Toho had decided Godzilla appealed to children and he is patronizing in every way a corporation can conceive. He's special friends with a latchkey kid and smoke ring blowing sidekick to Godzilla. The best thing I can say about Minilla is that he calls in to question Godzilla's sex.

That said, it is funny when, in 2004's *Godzilla: Final Wars*, Minilla's driven around in a Japanese lorry. The scene makes me think of the possibilities of Jim Jarmusch's *Godzilla*. John Lurie wouldn't like Minilla, but he'd give him a lift because someone had to. Lurie'd end up in a conversation with Ifukube Akira at some 24 hour diner while Minilla went off to stop Godzilla destroying the greater metropolitan area.

But Minilla and his radioactive smoke rings cloud the issue. Rubber suits are not off brand computer-generated special effects, they are puppetry. Confronted with a guy in a rubber suit, I suspend my disbelief right quick in a way I don't with computer generated monsters. Roland Emmerich's 1998 CG Godzilla forces me to confront its artificiality over and over. Every attempt to make the monster more plausible (it's a mutant komodo dragon), every little bit of scientific exposition (its atomizing breath is bacterial komodo breath), only kicks me out of the movie, especially since the "bad science" is part of the draw for me. I love the transparencies of Godzilla's cells and the crazy explanations of "regenerator g-1." Why make things less fun? Like Wittgenstein says, I like science as a manner of speaking. If you're looking for a film with realistic aliens and plausible science, go see *Contact*.

Every realistic explanation about something unreal requires another and Hollywood's Godzilla becomes all about justifying a giant monster's plausibility. It distracts from the heart of Godzilla movies. Godzilla is not about what a monster would be like in the real world. Godzilla represents an experience. Until the occupation ended in 1952, the U.S. military censored all representations of Hiroshima and Nagasaki. In fact, U.S. military footage of the cities was not released to the Japanese government, let alone the American public, until 1978. As far as I am concerned, if it's not about annihilation, it's not a Godzilla movie.

In Central and South America, writers used magical realism to write about terrifying political realities. Looking at Toho studio's monsters and armies, I ponder how puppetry trumps direct representation, capturing the simultaneous intentional and impersonal nature of the bombings, deliberate and caused by humans but too totally devastating to comprehend as anything but disaster.

Until a few weeks ago, I would've said that CG always threw me out of the movie, at least out of movies with giant monsters traditionally played by guys in rubber suits. But then I saw Bong Joon-Ho's *The Host* at the 2006 Toronto International Film Festival. The CG worked fine for a slippery river monster spawned from formaldehyde dumped into Seoul's Han River, on the orders of a U.S. military commander. What is it about it U.S. military actions that lend themselves to processing through giant monsters?

What part of that's a guy in a suit don't people understand? The guy in a suit is a metonym that stands for all the movie's implausible parts. The guy in a suit reminds us that Godzilla is about something else, maybe has more in common with magical realism or medieval morality plays than science fiction cinema, if you don't mind me going off half-cocked. If you can't get over Godzilla being a guy in a suit in the first five minutes, then you are missing the point. Honestly, why attack a genre for its conventions?

Love Song of the Black Lagoon

We have lingered in the chambers of the sea
By gillmen wreathed with seaweed red and brown
Till human voices wake us, and we drown.
—sorta T.S. Eliot[1]

Do you hear that? Off in the distance? A song too beautiful to be real but somehow... familiar? The song twines over the water, through the cattails and the woods, into the window, eighth notes swirling all around. The creature in the lagoon is singing. He's not dead after all and who are we to resist him and the "centuries of passion pent up in his savage heart?"[2]

Lilli Carré's *The Lagoon* centers on that song and the nameless family who hear it. It's hard to say what the creature's motivation is. Revenge? Love? Loneliness? And it's hard to say what's going on with the family, but something's ragged claws are scuttling beneath the surface. Maybe it's the creature. Maybe not. "What was it? Science didn't know, but dedicated scientists were willing to risk their lives to find out!" a trailer for *The Creature from the Black Lagoon* exclaims. Though I was dedicated, I never found out the family's secret, let alone their names.

Carré's book reads like an epilogue to Universal's 1950s horror trilogy: *The Creature from the Black Lagoon*, *Revenge of the Creature* and *The Creature Walks Among Us*. With its cinematic, swamp gothic feel, *The Lagoon* fits with the trilogy's arc—the gillman provoked in his paradise, displayed in an aquarium and finally operated on by a mad scientist, burning away the outer scales and revealing "a structure of human skin" to make the gillman more human.[3] Now the creature, if it is the same creature, lives in a swamp near a development.[4]

The Lagoon inverts a couple of *The Creature from the Black Lagoon*'s elements. In the film, an explorer drops her cigarette into the water, a Fall from Eden gesture that turns the gillman's Amazonian paradise into a scientist's ashtray. In The Lagoon, the creature returns the favor by flicking a still burning butt into a woodpile outside the family's house. And the creature not only smokes, he has an affair with the woman, who might be one of those women in the movies whose "beauty [had been] a lure to even a Man-Beast from the dawn of time" and led him to be shot, exhibited and experimentally altered.[5] This time, it's not the Man-Beast who's lured to his doom. Late at night, the creature sings and people stand in the water listening. Some of them drown.

Carré's choice to organize a silent medium around sound is an interesting one. She could've made a short film. She's made other ones. (You can see them at her website, www.lillicarre.com). Comics critic Glen Weldon writes that horror comics by their very nature defy a central horror tenet, "The scariest stuff is the stuff you don't see."[6] In *The Lagoon*, the most haunting and seductive song is the one we never hear. We see the song as a series of eighth notes winding through woods, whistled by grandpa or played on the piano by the daughter. But even in a film, the siren song we hear only represents the one that could drown us. Because she's working in a silent medium, Carré's never stuck with a siren song's conventions, which are usually soprano and operatic if sword and sandals movies are anything to go by. A song that lures us to our doom might be an aria, but it could also be something unconventionally beautiful or yearning, something like Tom Waits' falsetto in "Sea of Love." In a comic, it can be anything.

I can't help but have a vague sense of the creature's song as a scratchy old jazz record—an instrumental I can almost remember. Something half-heard. Seeing a song visually represented creates the sense of something on the verge of consciousness. And that sense of something half-remembered, half-conceived or half-understood is part of how I think the creature's song draws people. The family's humming, whistling, playing the piano, their attempts to recreate the song, maybe understand it, are part of the hook.

Horror like *The Creature from the Black Lagoon* isn't just shock, gore and endangered virtue; it's also about the unknown and the tragic, gradual realization of unbridgeable distance. The creature in *The Lagoon* is unknown and possibly unknowable to the people who exist beside it. Men listening in the weeds warn the woman's husband, "Who knows if the creature intended to drown people or if it just wanted someone to sing to and didn't know any better."

In one of his philosophical fortune cookies, Wittgenstein says something like, "If a gillman could talk, we couldn't understand him." In *The Lagoon*, that's the crux of the problem. So, sure, the song is a connection between the creature and the people, but his audience can't be sure they understand him. The woman has a relationship with the creature, but doesn't necessarily know how the creature understands that relationship. There is attachment and a song. The creature sings and humans feel.

But we never know what song will do us in.

1 Eliot, T.S. "The Love Song of J. Alfred Prufrock." Eds. Richard Ellmann and Robert O'Clair. The Norton Anthology of Modern Poetry: Second Edition. New York: W.W. Norton & Co., 1988: 482. Print.

2 "Taglines for The Creature from the Black Lagoon." IMDb.com. Internet Movie Database, n.d. Web. Mar. 2009. <http://www.imdb.com/title/tt0046876/taglines>

3 "The Creature Walks Among Us Trailer." YouTube.com. YouTube, n.d. Web. Mar. 2009. <http://www.youtube.com/watch?v=98qRt-DGuZ0>

4 If it's not the same creature, the issues would probably be the same: scientific experiments, exhibitions and the inescapable beauty of human ladies, especially white ladies.

5 "Taglines for The Creature from the Black Lagoon." IMDb.com. Internet Movie Database, n.d. Web. Mar. 2009. <http://www.imdb.com/title/tt0046876/taglines>

6 Weldon, Glen. "Funnybook Roundup, Halloween Edition: Braaaaaaaaaains...." Monkey See Blog. National Public Radio. NPR.org. 28 Oct. 2009. Web. March, 2009. <http://www.npr.org/blogs/monkeysee/2008/10/ funnybook_roundup_halloween_ed_1. html>

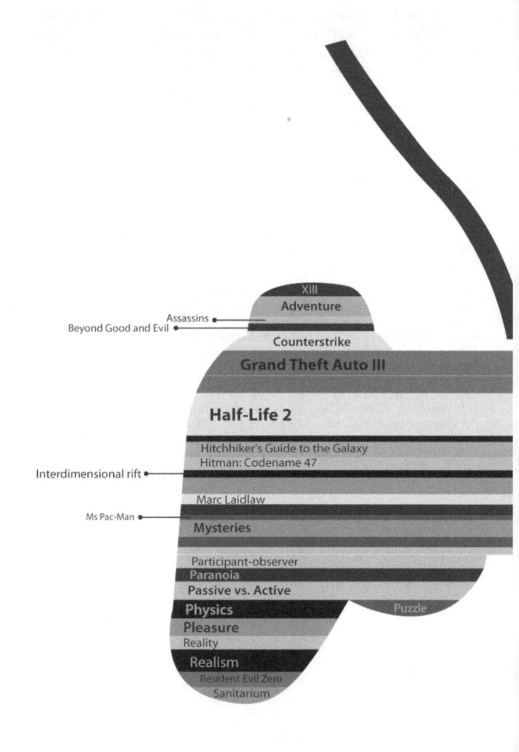

XIII

Adventure

Assassins

Beyond Good and Evil

Counterstrike

Grand Theft Auto III

Half-Life 2

Hitchhiker's Guide to the Galaxy
Hitman: Codename 47

Interdimensional rift

Marc Laidlaw

Ms Pac-Man

Mysteries

Participant-observer
Paranoia
Passive vs. Active

Physics

Pleasure

Reality

Realism

Resident Evil Zero
Sanitarium

Puzzle

GAMES

Jim Munroe

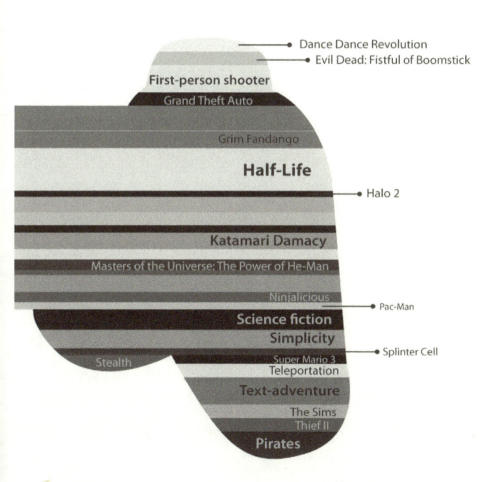

- Dance Dance Revolution
- Evil Dead: Fistful of Boomstick

First-person shooter

Grand Theft Auto

Grim Fandango

Half-Life

- Halo 2

Katamari Damacy

Masters of the Universe: The Power of He-Man

Ninjalicious

- Pac-Man

Science fiction

Simplicity

- Splinter Cell

Stealth

Super Mario 3

Teleportation

Text-adventure

The Sims

Thief II

Pirates

Is it Possible to Have Too Much Fun?

Is it possible to have a pleasure circuit *overload*?

"Girls are to be kept away from those activities of civilization that over-stimulate the imagination and the senses, such as fashionable novels, paintings, music, balls, theaters... as this can lead to uterine epilepsy, sapphic tastes, and nymphomania."

While this is Victorian-era advice, it's reflective of how certain people deal with something that's new and sexy: hysteria. It's the same people who are now blaming video games, today's over-stimulant of choice, for everything from obesity to mass murder. Even those of us who aren't concerned parents or members of the religious community have a tendency to look at video games as a waste of time when compared, say, to reading a novel.

As someone who makes his living from writing novels, let me tell you that this is sanctimonious horseshit.

There's no shortage of time-wasting novels, and plenty of brilliant videogames, and the dismissal of a medium in its infancy says volumes about the guilt we have about playing and pleasure. This snobbery prevents this hugely popular entertainment industry (a $13.5-billion annual gross revenue in the States alone places it ahead of Hollywood) from getting the critical focus it needs to grow. Despite the numbers proving that it fills a social need, there's next to no serious cultural discourse about it.

I'm not just talking about critical reviews or in-depth profiles, I'm talking about people chit-chatting at parties. While it's acceptable to discuss the cinematography in a movie you've just seen, try bringing up the inventive and creepy camera angles in *Resident Evil Zero* (Capcom). While you can recommend a page-turner to a total stranger without raising eyebrows, try recommending the brilliant *Grim Fandango* (LucasArts). Rueful grins and shaking heads are all you'll get.

Why? Well, like porn, there's something naked about the fantasy-fulfillment most video games offer—you can drive that big rig, shoot that terrorist and hit that ball in a way you never could in real life—that seems basically juvenile. Like science fiction, comics and other gutter genres, playing video games is something kids do.

And more often than not, people have had some unsatisfying experience with one kind of game and dismissed them as a whole. That's like dismissing the world of film based on watching an action flick. Because there is very little discussion about games, there's no vocabulary to describe how the experience was unsatisfying, and consequently find a type of game you might like better. While you might come away from a boring movie and say that the pace was too slow or that the acting was wooden, when most people quit playing games they don't tend to say that the cut scenes were too talky or the interface was cluttered.

The medium as a whole has a much more inbred feedback loop than those that continually strengthen and stimulate the legit media. Hardcore gamers, the most vocal feedbackers game designers have, are often more impressed by more realistically rendered lava than cohesive storylines or intriguing characters.

So it becomes a vicious circle: designers aren't given much incentive to raise the bar except technologically, and consequently the potential next-generation designers don't find much to inspire them to pursue a career in videogame-making. Without the "I wanna make a game/movie/album like 'X,'" it's hard to keep the spark alive in any medium.

But plenty have pushed the medium in interesting directions. Because they don't really know where it will go, it can be both exciting and frightening. While wandering freely around the aptly named Liberty City of *Grand Theft Auto III* (Rockstar Games), I was struck by how the most accessible and realistically detailed virtual city thus far created was not made by an urban planning thinktank or architectural company, but as a byproduct of a first-person shooter. And since the odds are that we'll be spending more and more time in virtual environments in the coming decades (email's the thin end of the wedge), what will it mean for us to have had our first experiences be psychopathic killing sprees? As fun as those sprees are, they're only one fantasy among many that could be played out.

Compelling games and the questions they pose are what I'm going to focus on for this column. From the weeks solid I spent as a teenager unravelling text-adventure games to the hours I spent finishing Grand Theft Auto III last night, I've been engaged and excited by games - sometimes from afar, as there was a 10-year drought in between when I filled the void with art and politics. This mix gives me a sympathetic but critical eye on the medium, makes me a participant-observer if you will, and I aim to temper my enthusiasm with analysis of both the game itself and its place in our society.

Video Games: The Timewasting Junk That's Changing Our Culture.

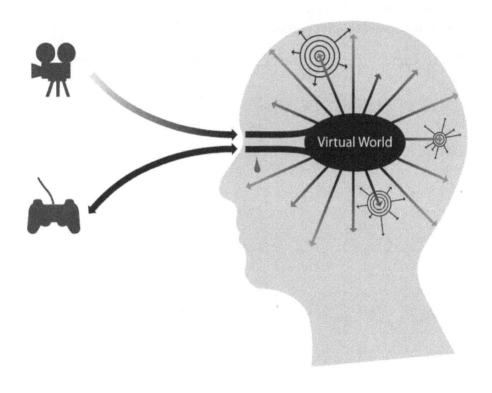

When Reality Bleeds

Two ravers are discussing how ridiculous it is that videogames are blamed for inciting killing sprees. "Yeah," one says to the other. "We grew up playing *Pac-Man*, and it's not like we're running around in the dark, popping pills, and listening to repetitive electronic music."

This internet joke is funny on one level, but vaguely unsettling on another. Have we been affected by videogames in ways we're not even aware of? Obviously our culture has been affected by videogames, but do games have a lasting subliminal impact on an individual's intellectual and emotional self?

Of course they do.

In a post on gamegirladvance.com, "Play=Life in GTA3," the author describes how much playing *Grand Theft Auto 3* (Rockstar Games, 2001) has affected the risks she takes while driving. The scores of "me too!" comments after the article is testament to how common the feeling is.

I was walking down the street and I noticed a store was selling silver jewellery. It occurred to me that I needed silver, but I couldn't remember for what. *Ah yes, to close the interdimensional rift.* I had been playing *Evil Dead: Fistful of Boomstick* (THQ, 2003), and I'd learned that I needed to find silver to close the vortices to stop the hordes of zombies. If it had been a magic crystal, I probably wouldn't have put it in the same memory slot -- but as it was, "silver" was beside bus tickets, bread and orange juice in my mental shopping list.

Horrified yet?

A lot of gamers downplay the moments when their virtual worlds bleed into their reality. They realize it makes them sound Columbine. And even if they love games, they're often a little freaked out by their own brains. That's a shame, because if they looked at it closely they'd realize that there's lots of things that are just as affecting.

When people talk about how affecting a movie is, they mean it as a compliment. "It changed the way I look at baseball," says a sap leaving *Field of Dreams*. *Fight Club* was very good to boxing gyms.

For a long time, I had the opinion that if a movie affected me it was ipso facto a good movie. Then I saw *Bad Lieutenant*.

On my way home after the movie, which features Harvey Keitel as a seedy police officer, I looked around at my fellow subway passengers with different eyes. Everyone seemed fallen, suspect, nauseating. Certainly the movie affected me powerfully, and I'm not going to argue whether that made it better art (that's another discussion). I just know that I didn't like it.

I had a similar experience when I was playing *Hitman: Codename 47* (Eidos Interactive, 2000). You awake without memory, in a hospital. A disembodied voice trains you in the way of the knife and gun, and dispatches you to assassinate a variety of targets.

As a tall, bald westerner, you perhaps aren't the best choice to silently murder the heads of two rival triad gangs, but that's your mission. You garrotte the limo driver when he takes a piss in an alley and dress in his uniform to accomplish this. Your mission also states that you have to make it look like they killed each other -- and that's only the beginning of the disembodied voice's plan. After a few levels of being his tool, I felt too greasy to go on.

While these "realistic" depictions of corrupt and venal killers are a justifiable reaction against the squeaky-clean action hero who always kills with moral backing, the question remains: how much grit can you stomach in your media diet? Continuing that metaphor, what appetite you have for a certain type of media is also reflective of you, not just of the medium that's taking the heat.

But movies are passive and games are active, you say, there's a big difference.

We're used to the pitfalls of passive entertainment while interactivity still seems deadly and exotic. Everyone who isn't addicted to television craves movies, and so there's a consensus that staring at something for hours on end is normal. I think this difference between active and passive entertainment is like the difference between talking and listening: just doing one all the time gives you a skewed view of the world. It's also important to note that the excitement around first-person shooters doesn't come from nowhere—it owes a lot to the fact that you get to "be" the action hero from movies, a medium that's nurtured the fascination with gunplay and power for so long that it goes nearly unnoticed nowadays.

The designer of *Pac-Man*(Midway, 1980), when he wasn't secretly plotting the invention of the rave subculture, had pretty lofty ambitions when it came to the future of video games. In the wake of its popularity, Toru Iwatani was asked what he wanted to do next. He said that he'd like to make a game that makes people cry. When a videogame does affect mass culture in this subtle way, it will be a profound moment. One that will mirror the undocumented moment when, for the first time, sniffles were heard in the darkness of a movie theatre.

My Wicked Moves, Quantified

I love to dance. This always seems to come as a surprise to people, me with my big gangly 6'3" frame and all, but I quickly qualify: "Oh, I'm not *good* at dancing—I just love to dance."

It all started at a grade seven school mixer in 1985.

Our classroom, once the lights were flicked and a discoball was plugged in, was transformed. I was surrounded by the few friends I had at the time in a dark room, without even a beer to pose with as we leaned against the desks that had been moved against the wall.

Chris Beharry, a Guyanese kid who'd introduced me to this music his American cousins were listening to the year before—"It's called *rap* music"—was bopping his head. And eventually, his legs and arms followed suit.

I have no idea why I thought I could do the same, not being a particularly confident kid, but I did. I remember the exhilaration, not from the freedom of the movement itself (that came later) but rather the fact that no one was laughing at me. Despite my rather shaky popularity, the moves I was busting were not singled out for ridicule. After a while I took a break, wandered over to the snack table and enjoyed a potato chip, calmly surveying my boogying classmates from the heights of my new social standing.

Since that triumphant moment, whenever I find myself in a club or at a wedding or anywhere else where the normal rules are suspended in favour of dancing to cheesy breakbeat anthems or hip-hop, I'm usually shaking what I got. Once, very drunk in a club on a cruiseboat headed for Helsinki, I vowed to dance in every big city of the world— and I was only partially joking. So the idea of a videogame named *Dance Dance Revolution* may seem ludicrous to some, but it doesn't to me.

DDR, as it's known to its legions of fans, is a series of games from Konami that use a footpad in the place of a joystick. On the screen are a cascade of arrows (up, down, right, left) that scroll to the top in quick succession. When they get to a specific spot, the player foots the corresponding arrow and gets points based on how accurate their timing was. A quantification of rhythm, if not grace. It's all done, of course, to a fabulous dance favourite booming out of the most sophisticated piece of electronics on the game unit: the speakers.

The series has been around since 1998, and I'd seen the game in action plenty of times in Asia and in the Asian malls around Toronto. A quick spin on the internet will introduce you to fansites like ddrfreak.com that document the DDR competitions held in North American cities. But on a recent trip to a friend's Georgian Bay cottage I happened upon a beachfront arcade and was delighted to see that the revolution had spread as far as Tiny, Ontario.

It was time for me to stop denying myself. Slipping in a loonie (the new millennium's quarter), I chose "It's Raining Men" and got down to it. It took me a few seconds to figure out when I was supposed to foot the pad, so I got a "Miss!" and even a "Boo!" or two before I found my feet. But pretty soon I was nailing the arrows with the right rhythm, and even managed to do a right-left combo arrow—a leg-splitter—without missing a beat.

It was almost as fun to watch my friends dance. In between offering helpful hints, I chatted up the teenaged girls who were waiting their turn. "So what song do you like to play?" They mumbled something, and I said "Eh?" like the grandpa I was. "Blow My Whistle," one of them repeated emotionlessly, staring ahead at the screen. They had on matching white jackets festooned with a logo I believe I've seen in *Vice* magazine.

When the two teenaged girls took the stage—which they could, since there were two footpads side by side—we shamelessly looked on. They indeed chose the song they had said, except that its full name (wisely truncated) was "Blow My Whistle, Bitch." Their synchronized dancing would have been more impressive except for the multitudes of "Miss!" and "Boos!" the screen gave them. We floated away, trying not to show the girls how disappointed we were in them, when another young lady took the stage.

She wasn't as pretty or as stylishly dressed as the other two, but you could tell by the way she whipped through the menus that she was a pro. While her song played, she hit all the arrows and then some, and the arrows were flying a mite bit faster than they had been with us. Between levels she adjusted her hoodie and gave the audience a whatchulookinat kind of glare. Then she went back to dancing, staring at the screen, her feet flying and self-conscious not in the slightest.

Sure, the other girls had the money and the boys. But at the end of the day, who had the fuckin' high score?

The Cultural Gutter

Mission: Look at Neat Stuff

Ninjalicious is the founder of *Infiltration*, a zine documenting his urban exploration hobby in hilarious and diagram-enhanced travelogues. He's recently been playing *Thief II* (Eidos, 2000), a videogame with a focus on stealth, and I asked him about how the first-person sneaker measured up to his real-life experience.

What made you start playing it?

I thought it would be cool to see if it could be used as practice, or at least to check out if it was realistic. I wouldn't go as far as to say it can be used as practice, but it's pretty realistic.

Yeah, a lot of the game is about listening—you can hear people's footfalls in the game. How close is that experience to what you do?

Obviously it lacks some subtlety—in real life, if you concentrate on your footfalls you won't make any noise on any surface, but in the game it's impossible to walk across a metal catwalk silently. But the game does teach you to favour grass and carpet over tile and wood. Some of the other sounds they've chosen to ignore are kind of weird. It doesn't make any noise to open and close a door—it makes a sound, but the guard doesn't "hear" it.

What else would you like to see?

More dead ends. In real life there are lots. I guess it's kind of frustrating in a videogame, but...

I've noticed that. Everything's there for a reason. When I come across a flippable switch in any game, I flip it.

See, in real life I would never pull a switch like that. It'd be trouble. I like to be careful. I get a kick out of being really careful. They've put a lot of time into this game but I'd admire them if they were willing to have a few useless things, a few dead ends.

Videogames never try to teach you how to know when to give up. While everything is there for a purpose, what I noticed with one of the levels was that I was able to achieve the objective without going through a third of the rooms.

To me that's admirable, because they know that some people are going to push right through it. I did do everything on that level, just for the sake of seeing everything.

Shouldn't they force you to get to know every level well?

No! The game is best when you're in unfamiliar territory. The best game of *Thief II* I had was my first—exploring the building without realizing that I was able to do anything other than sneak and hide, and not having any clue what the various threats were. As you play the game you realize, oh, the AI is not that smart—the guards just walk back and forth in a pattern.

The artificial intelligence is patchy.

Yeah. One of the major innovations that *Ms Pac-Man* (Midway, 1981) made over *Pac-Man* (Midway, 1980) was that the ghosts stopped simply predictably chasing your character and threw in some random stuff as well. There needs to be more of that with these guards.

Given the choice, a human opponent is more satisfying?

Yeah. The game and real life are similar in that you're trying to figure out a puzzle and people are pieces in that puzzle, but in *Thief II* I would say the most interesting pieces are architectural or mechanical while in real life the most interesting pieces are people.

Puzzle? Give me a real-life example.

Well, like getting in the pool in the Crown Plaza Hotel. The door was locked, and it was a glass door, and there was always an attendant at the desk. You couldn't wait at the door, because they'd see you waiting there. What you had to do was go down the hallway, wait until you heard the elevator ding, then you'd have to walk down the hallway, getting your pace just right so you'd arrive at the same time as the person who had a key. You had to make small talk with the person as you went through so it looked like you were buddies.

That is such a videogame moment.

I was well aware of that at the time. I was like, 'Oh yeah, this is better than *Impossible Mission* or *Elevator Action*.'

I noticed that the infiltration.org site used to have an *Elevator Action* theme—how much of your hobby comes from videogames?

About half. Half comes from *2600*, the magazine about hacking, and half comes from videogame cheat books. Playing the game was fun, but reading the cheat books was really fun. I wanted to write cheat books for exploring real places.

Final comments?

I get a real kick out of there not only being rooftops to explore, but drains and boiler rooms. But if it was up to me, the only goal would be to take pictures of these things and leave.

The Name Game

While I wait in the lobby of one of the largest game studios in the world, I watch someone go through to the inner sanctum. The shiny barrier, with transparent doors that whir apart at the wave of a card-pass, looks familiar—I think I've seen the devices being used as turnstiles in a Tokyo subway.

Most places of work are satisfied with a locked door, but someone at Ubisoft Montreal decided they needed something with a little more panache. Something that made the employees feel important and impressed visitors. And something that said, "No, you won't just be waltzing in here and stealing our secrets."

I half-wonder if I'm being tested.

After all, the company's breakthrough title was *Splinter Cell*, a military stealth game in which you circumvent much more challenging security than this. And last year's *Beyond Good and Evil* has you sneaking around taking photos of sensitive information in order to topple a corrupt government.

But before I become convinced that the office is a set piece in some kind of real-life metagame upon which my life depends, Tali arrives. She welcomes me, swipes me through the subway turnstile, and shows me around. I'd just asked to have a look at the place while I was in town, maybe chat with some of the people who made the games. Most of the rooms are cubicle-style, open-concept kind of areas filled with a bunch of average-looking guys. What they have on their screens is different depending on whether they are play-testing, modelling, animating or producing the games, but their slumped posture and dispirited mouse-clicking are pretty much office-worker-standard for a Friday afternoon.

We continue on another floor, and Tali's commentary pauses as we pass another clump of cubicles. Then she says, "Can't tell you what's going on there." I naturally cast my eyes over this forbidden zone, but nothing stands out as notably different. I'm amused by it on the one hand—damn, and me without my lapel-pin spy camera!—and also slightly irritated.

A lot of the game world is top secret and hush-hush. Non-disclosure agreements are flying all over the place. Everyone from play-testers to journalists is asked to sign them, and you can almost understand in those cases. But when you make someone keep quiet about what they do for most of their waking hours, are you asking too much? And ethics aside, when so many great ideas happen through casual conversation in off-hours, is this even an effective way to run a creative business?

As we wait for the elevator, I ask Tali about the secrecy that pervades the videogame industry. "I mean, you don't see it in the movies as much..."

She thinks about it. "Well, they rely a lot on pre-publicity..." she says. "Plus, if they have Tom Cruise acting in their movie, it's not like you can steal that in the same way you can steal an idea for a game."

The "marquee name" power that certain actors and directors have in film is not that common in videogames. Brands and game titles have always had the limelight (Atari, *Pac-Man*, etc.) and not the creators behind them. This is despite long-term pressure for the humans behind the games to get some credit. Arnie Katz wrote in the June, 1983 *Electronic Games* magazine, "All designers of electronic games are just as much creative artists as painters and novelists.... Why shouldn't the creator of such a work of art be entitled to put his or her name on it to reap the praise and brickbats of gaming consumers?"

As a result of this, the Intellivision and Atari 2600 cartridges of *Masters of the Universe: The Power of He-Man* had the design teams credited on the packaging. But even He-Man could only push it so far -- today, though credits rolling at the end of a game are common, games haven't made the big step towards the marquee name. I bring this up with Tali, and she points to a promotional cutout picture of *XIII*, a game done in a graphic novel style with voice acting by David Duchovny and Adam West.

I admit that having the voice of Batman encourage me along was one of my favourite parts of *XIII*, but it's different when the names attached to the game have star power in other media. Once game makers promote the designers and the art directors, audiences will start picking up games based on those things... and the industry will have its own marquee names native to the form.

Sure, it'll spawn a few *enfants terribles*. It's not like a superstar designer won't make games just as crappy as a game company on its own, but being able to raise funds for a game based on, say, having a prominent art director attached, will mean more diversity in how games can be made.

You can steal bits and pieces of a project, but a good game is more than the sum of its parts. The secrecy and paranoia belies an adolescent lack of confidence in this, a lack of trust that your audience won't know a rip-off from the genuine quality article. All these electromagnetic doors, arcane contracts and press leaks—they're good cloak-and-dagger fun and all, but it's time to grow up.

How to Spoil a Game

You wake up in a centuries-old asylum. Your face is in bandages and your memory is in tatters, only coming back to you in black and white cinematic flashes. As you walk around and talk to people, you solve puzzles and unearth the mystery of your identity, travelling to different places that may only exist in your mind.

Sanitarium (DreamForge, 1998) is a puzzle-based adventure game for the PC, and playing the game caused me to stumble across another mystery from my own past: why does taking hints when I'm stuck in a game ruin it for me?

The appeal of games like *Sanitarium* is not in their realism. *Sanitarium*'s got what's known as a semi-isometric, top-down view, which will be a familiar one for players of *The Sims*. When you make your character go into a room, the top dissolves with a ghostly sound and reveals what's inside, reminiscent of a dollhouse. The miniature characters are slightly blurred and unreal, which suits the creepy tone. When you encounter mutated children, their varied characters come through in their voices (tremulous, nasty) rather that the glimpse you're given of their twisted faces.

The way that environments are small—as opposed to the sprawling, free-form settings of a lot of 3-D shooters—is actually preferable in a puzzle game like this. When you have a half-dozen rooms rather than a hundred, you'll more easily find the stick on the ground that you need to poke the pig so it runs and gets rid of the dog, which allows you to get through the garden to the gazebo...

That's not a real solution to anything, by the way, but that's the kind of sequential list of things you do to progress in *Sanitarium*. When you come across something, you know you'll be using it later—again, not realistic, but the interlocking tasks are fun to set in motion. Like the Rube Goldbergian contraptions that start by pushing over a domino that turns on a fan that blows up a balloon, there's a satisfaction in getting it right.

But there's an equal frustration in getting it wrong. In chapter two of *Sanitarium*, I got stuck. I knew what I needed to do but I couldn't find the thing I needed to do it with. So I spent a few hours pixel-picking—

revisiting everywhere I could, scrolling my mouse over everything that looked like it might be takeable. I knew the environment pretty well because earlier, the kids in the game had played a game of hide-and-seek with me, so I had to find them—a great little interlude where you have to watch carefully for the motion of someone peeking out of their hiding spot.

But this game of hide-and-seek was less fun, and I started to worry that the game might be buggy. So I searched the internet, found that there were no relevant bugs—and also found some hints. And I should have known better, but I looked.

When I was 15 and stumped by *The Hitchhiker's Guide to the Galaxy* (Infocom, 1984), we didn't have the internet, so I bought the official *InvisiClues* hint book. I took but one hint but to this day I've never really felt like I finished that game myself. It's a great game but my experience of it is somehow tainted by never really knowing if I could have completed it without help. Since that time, I've never taken hints. I've let games sit, come back to them months, or sometimes years, later, and give them another try—and more often than not, I figure it out eventually.

When I wrote my own text adventure, *Punk Points*, I didn't include any hints, nor do I give any to people who ask. It's not to be mean, it's just because I've learned the correlation between challenge and satisfaction. When I write books, I'm more concerned about making things clearer—starting subtle, and moving towards obviousness if I need to—but with a game I'm OK with a smaller, more intense audience.

With *Sanitarium*, I had decided that as a reviewer I should take a hint—I didn't want to recommend a game that was buggy or impossible, did I?—and I thought that I might have changed in the 15 years since I took my last hint. I don't take games as seriously now as I did then, when I might have had a passionate opinion about whether hints were cheating and took unironic pride in completing a game.

But the thing that I was stuck on wasn't a bug, or impossible, and instead was something I would have figured out in time. And now... I find that my enthusiasm for the game has dissipated. It feels like watching a movie with a twist ending that I know about beforehand. Good though it is, I doubt I'll go back to play it.

You'd think I would have gotten the hint the first time.

The Scientist-Hero Returns

I was a little nervous as I waited for *Half-Life 2* (Vivendi, 2004) to start. The original *Half-Life* (Sierra, 1998) is one of the reasons this column exists—the game brought atmosphere and intelligence to the first-person shooter without skimping on the visceral kickassocity, and brought me back to videogames after a decade of neglect.

The sequel had been talked up in the gaming community for years, and even being over a year late hadn't destroyed the enthusiasm. (Though coming out at the same time as *Halo 2* [Microsoft, 2004] did destroy the chance of mainstream press attention—the much less interesting game on Microsoft's Xbox console was backed by much more marketing money.) We remembered being Gordon Freeman, the scientist in the hazmat suit—a hero in glasses, for Christ's sake—having to shoot himself out of the Black Mesa lab turned horrific by an inter-dimensional snafu. We were willing to wait.

The loading screen is a good sign. A hazy blur of colour and shapes, evocative and mysterious, eventually sharpens into a street scene with the title and menu options overlaid. It's either twilight or pre-dawn, with cobblestones and architecture hinting at a European setting. There's a clicking of heels and a soldier in a face mask comes into the shot, doing his rounds. Then a flying sentry whirrs by, its steady bleeping not quite breaking the ominous silence.

That's just the menu screen. I choose Play New Game, a good deal of my nervousness having dissipated. The game begins aboard a train just pulling into City 17. I don't really know why I'm here, and I walk around the grandly decrepit train station listening as the video screens broadcast a welcome by a bearded man speaking calmly about "relocations" and "our benefactors." A man hunched at a lunch table throws a bag on the ground in disgust, and I approach him for information.

When I stand beside him, he looks at me. I'm a little surprised— I'm used to feeling like a pair of disembodied eyes in videogames, a point-of-view rather than a person. Gordon doesn't really speak, so the interaction with people isn't really a gameplay element—but it is effectively used to tell the story.

And there is a good story in *Half-Life 2*. Marc Laidlaw, who also wrote the predecessor, was a science-fiction novelist (*Kalifornia, The Orchid Eater*) before he started working with Valve. Both games have SF plots that, while not stunningly original, are told with subtlety and attention to detail. More importantly, they're adapted to the medium. I still remember playing the beginning of *Half-Life*, where I was told by a senior scientist to push a cart into the centre of the chamber. When I did this, I hit something and a disaster ensued—and I remember thinking, "Shit, I should have saved the game, now I'll have to start over"—but there's no way to avoid it. It was a brilliant method to make the player complicit in the "things-go-horribly awry" stock science-fiction plot. Far more engaging than just explaining in a cut scene that an interdimensional rift caused yadda yadda yadda.

And while there are parts in the game where the story is advanced, they're not the conventional sit-and-watch cut scenes. I could, for instance, run around the lab opening things while my fellow scientist explains the importance of the teleportation device to the underground resistance. The facial expressions and body language are remarkable and the dialogue is also a cut above. As he upgrades my swamp boat with a gun turret that came from the same model of 'copter that is chasing me, my comrade says "I like a little irony in my firefights."

I use the swamp boat to get to the outskirts of City 17, loath though I am to leave a city where I once glimpsed a giant H.G. Wellsian robot stalking by on towering insectile legs. But the detail lavished on the urban centre, even down to the style of graffiti and stencilled posters, is also extended to the outreaches of the city. You get a sense of the scale of the city as you speed down rivers that curve forever, flanked by electrical towers, bleak apartment buildings and factories.

My appreciation of the game will have to continue in in the second half of this article. I'm not the fastest game player, I know that for a fact: I recently ran across an announcement that David "Marshmallow" Gibbons had posted proof that he was able to finish *Half-Life 2* in two hours, 57 minutes. "Speed demos," as they're called, are done for many games and are backed up by video proof... the *Super Mario 3* one made waves last year.

As for me, I don't want to rush. I'm planning to savour the experience, spend some more time in beautifully crafted dystopias like City 17. *Half-Life 2* ends with a monologue by the mysterious G-Man, who's appeared through the entire game with his distinctive briefcase— ducking into a doorway, walking along a platform in the distance— always one step ahead of you. He looks fairly human, but the way his voice sounds like it's been spliced together (and the way he seems to be able to stroll between dimensions and stop time) suggest something more unworldly. The ending monologue intimates that he's not above selling your services to the highest bidder, but it was the phrase "illusion of free will" that caught my ear.

As a novelist, I strive for verisimilitude: the appearance of reality. I try to give a sense of place, a person's life, a situation, not by giving exhaustive descriptive detail but by giving just enough detail to evoke a feeling of realism. The videogame has to do this with the visuals and the narrative, but faces an additional challenge: giving people the illusion of free will.

People sometimes criticize the *Half-Life* series for being "on a rail"— more or less like a funhouse ride on which you're shuttled through constructed scenarios. Having tight control like this is a trade-off for a nuanced and complex narrative. In opposition to this, games in the *Grand Theft Auto* series offer scenarios, rather than stories, and are often referred to as "sandbox games." While both limit the player's free will, they employ different strategies of evoking the illusion of maintaining it.

Half-Life 2 does this through a steady diet of marvels, a lot of them based on how smart the objects are. If, in a moment of panic, you grab a nearby paint can and throw it at a zombie, the zombie will be covered in paint. If you grab a circular saw and throw it, the zombie will be sliced in two (and if you go to look, you will see the saw half-embedded in the wall behind). Shoot someone with a crossbow and they will hang literally pinned to the wall. Physics are used a lot in puzzles—if you weigh down one end of a see-saw with the concrete debris lying around, you can get up to the second level. At another part, the buoyancy of plastic barrels in water comes into play.

But the shock of recognition (my god, it's rolling down the hill like a real tire would!) that is a big part of the appeal of physics is only one possible use of these complex mathematical algorithms. Unlike the physics in our world, gameworld physics aren't natural laws— they're as changeable as the visual environments. And *Half-Life 2* takes admirable advantage of this, drawing on its futuristic setting to introduce the gravity gun.

With the gravity gun—a.k.a. the zero-point energy field manipulator— you can suck objects into the field, have them hover in front of you, and then fire them away at great force. The gravity gun is quite a unique weapon—even the alien weapons of some games simply exchange energy bolts for bullets and don't really have their own character. With the gravity gun you can pick up filing cabinets and shoot them at oncoming soldiers. Need something below on the cavern floor infested with vicious head crabs? Reverse its gravity and watch it come to you. Out of grenades? Hurl a barrel of gasoline at an ant-lion and watch it explode on impact, then watch the animal thrash around in flames until it finally collapses.

Speaking of ant-lions, when you're on the coastline, these buggers appear from under the sand and attack you relentlessly. But once you kill one of their mothers, you're able to harvest the pheromone sacks. Now they're under your control, and you can call them from the sands and direct them to harass your enemies.

You find a less successful variant on the pheromone-sack weapon when you're fighting in the city, and word of your heroic actions has spread to the point that the resistance humans you meet all want to fight with you. You can direct them into battle like the ant-lions, and they'll run off to get killed. But unlike the ant-lions I remorselessly sent into battle and watched from a distance, I felt like I had to lead the charge for my human squad. I didn't really need their help, where elsewhere in the game (the gun turret scene in "Entanglement"), I was stuck for hours. They died very quietly and everything, but mostly they just got in the way (constantly saying stuff like, "Excuse me, Dr. Freeman," "Let me get out of your way, Dr. Freeman") as I plowed through the bombed-out buildings of City 17.

Dr. Freeman is better as a loner, not a soldier. This becomes apparent as you drive across the beached coastline about halfway through the game, which has a melancholy feel of a post-apocalyptic road trip. A soldier busts out of an outpost and you gun him down before he can do the same to you. You go into the little tin shack he came out of to scavenge supplies. But there're no medkits or ammo, just the soldier's belongings and the old mattress he slept on.

Rolling Pleasure

In a brief flashback to the hip Queen Street West I remember from the '80s, I chanced upon a cult-hit videogame there. I was killing time and wandered into Microplay and asked the counter guy if any interesting games had come down the pike lately. "Yeah," he said, "There's this Japanese game…" He passed me a PlayStation 2 game with a curiously static image on the cover: a cow standing in a field next to a gigantic ball of… stuff. I made a mental note of the name: Katamari Damacy (Namco, 2004).

"You roll that ball around," he explained. "And if you roll up enough stuff it gets put up into the sky and becomes a star." I suppose I looked baffled, because he shrugged and said, "I haven't played it yet, but people really love it."

When I eventually got the game, I found out why. It's a refreshingly simple and fun arcade-style game. With its amazing soundtrack and psychedelic rainbow visuals it captivates shroom-head adults and sugar-high kids alike. You begin the game a few millimetres tall, rolling around a ball on a desk and picking up thumbtacks and ants, until your ball is big enough to pick up bigger objects. If you keep on rollin', eventually you're picking up cars and cows and even people. The apt title of the sequel, scheduled for release in Japan this spring, is *Everyone Loves Katamari*.

Keita Takahashi knew what he was doing when he designed the game. Takahashi, at the Game Developers' Conference held in San Francisco this past March, talked about how he intended for it to be loved, that he wanted to create something "enjoyable and funny." That's not to say that he didn't have deeper thoughts than that: he followed it up by pointing out that the flipside to violent games inspiring violence is that pleasurable games can inspire pleasure. This was well received by an audience of game developers who can hardly ignore that videogames are our culture's latest bogeyman, simultaneously regarded as a waste of time and all-powerful influence.

Takahashi's talk was the highlight of the GDC for me. I caught a glimpse of him the night before accepting awards for game design and innovation in art-school slacker clothes, and I had worried that the talk would be a lot of him shrugging and being charming. (That's not so awful, just not worth getting up for at 9am.) But he was a very generous and candid speaker, bringing up ideas like love and punk alongside practical ways the industry can improve, all while doodling the Prince and the King on his desktop.

Translated via headphones from the Japanese, he showed us some of the work he did while going to school for sculpture. Among them were a coffee table that transformed into a flying robot and a goat-shaped flowerpot, which went a long way to explaining the whimsy and spatial use in *Katamari Damacy*. That he had an arts background made a lot of sense to me too, because the kitschy-cool-crazy-Japanese feel of the game seemed too self-aware to be solely the product of a game company.

And while Namco did release the game, the objects in it were built by students in a computer graphics design class assigned it as a project. That explained the specificity of the objects—there's a learner's permit, for instance. It also pointed at another possibility for game development beyond the game company model. Takahashi himself is an interesting manifestation of the game auteur that is becoming more and more linked to innovation and breakthrough games: unlike many of his auteur predecessors, who are compared to movie directors, he's drawing from other artistic wells.

Takahashi also showed the original prototype for the game, which was almost identical to the final game. In getting his vision through the game company system intact, Takahashi admitted that he had to "proactively ignore" pressure to make the game (which famously only uses the two analogue sticks of the PS2's multitude of buttons) more complex. In the Q&A there was a question about whether changing the name from the Japanese (pronounced "katamari dama-she," by the way, and roughly translating as "clump soul") was ever considered for the Western market. Takahashi said no.

Not that Takahashi is unconcerned with how the game is marketed. In his talk, he addressed the fact that in Japan, where gaming is often thought by Westerners to be more acceptable, there's still a stigma. "Gamers are the ones who buy games," he said. To combat this, he suggested that manuals could be created for games that were as well designed and intriguing as books in bookstores. People who would be too intimidated to pick up a controller for a demo in a game store might flip through a book.

While this could easily be dismissed as a packaging gimmick to bring in more money, it's actually idealism. Takahashi is applying the same intentions to promotion and marketing that he's applied to making the game: reaching out to non-gamers and bringing them pleasure. It's a kind of advocacy that has faith in the transformative power of gaming, rather than insisting that gaming be taken seriously.

Makes me wonder if Takahashi very roughly translates to "he who offers the stick-of-joy."

Rethinking Brain Eating

If he feels vindicated, he doesn't show it. As Marc Laidlaw waits for his co-workers to finish a talk, we sit down at a table in San Francisco's cavernous Moscone Center and talk about *Half-Life 2* (Valve, 2004).

Its 1998 predecessor is legendary for pushing the form both narratively (bringing atmosphere and intelligence to the first-person shooter) and technologically (the *Half-Life* engine having been used for the online phenomenon *Counterstrike*). As if living up to that wasn't enough, the sequel took six years to make and was plagued by delays and a code leak of a beta version of the game. But I meet up with Marc the day after the first-person shooter game has swept the Game Developers Choice Awards: it won Best Game, Technology, Character Design and Writing.

As indicated by the last two awards, Laidlaw's background as a novelist (he got into games through writing *Wired* articles about the game company that made *Doom*) has given him a skill for character development rarely seen in the industry. He explains how he approaches the dramatic scenes in the game: "In the same way we set about designing an ambush with some monsters, we're going to design a scene where we want a specific emotional impact. For instance, the scene where you first get to Eli's lab, we wanted you to feel like you were watching a family dynamic with this daughter-and-stepmother kind of energy going on," Laidlaw says.

Perhaps because he's confident about his writing, he's learned the difficult art of what not to say. "I'm not a big fan of too much dialogue; it needs to be just enough. But we tend to overwrite and record a lot of extra stuff that we don't use, and then it's kind of like scaffolding. Because as soon as you have communicated enough to the animators, they're able to express a lot of it non-verbally and we can cut the scene down further and just communicate more visually. And it's a visual medium."

That was something I'd forgotten when I asked the publishers of *Half-Life 2: Raising the Bar* (Prima Games, 2004) to send me a review copy. For some reason, I'd expected a non-fiction account of the making of the game, but what arrived was a lavish coffee-table book featuring examples of the visually stunning work of the game accompanied by 100-word descriptions. What comes across in the book, which quotes dozens of people, is how much collaboration shaped the process.

Laidlaw explains that this was the case even with the dialogue, which could have been solely the domain of the writer. "We basically created radio plays, and we'd get a bunch of extra stuff: 'Let's try this line. You're doing this line really close up; now you're 20 feet away; you're angry; you're scared.' We'll take that stuff back to the lab, and these are our pieces for building the scene. And then in the process of that, we'll usually find little weird bits and pieces in the outtakes and the alternates that will inspire one of the animators."

And Laidlaw says it helped that there were a couple of pairs of ears cocked for inspiration. "Like in Eli's lab, when he's kind of teasing you and Alyx, and he goes 'Awwwwyyyyiii!' Well, that's just the sound [voice actor] Robert [Guillaume] made. When Bill Fletcher and I were going through the audio stuff, we just heard this sound, and we were like, 'Oh, we gotta use that sound.' Bill instantly saw something to do with it, and so he took it away and fed it into the scene. It wasn't supposed to be there, but as soon as we heard it, it had to be there. It was just such an interesting sound."

Laidlaw says trusting what he finds interesting is key to working with a genre many consider hackneyed. "A lot of science-fiction stuff works in games because it hasn't been done before in a game, although it's been done to death in every other medium. In the first game it was the cliché of the trans-dimensional teleporter; this one has the cliché of the Orwellian future. We're always on the lookout for the science-fiction clichés... They're good because everybody recognizes them and you don't have to explain them before you turn them on their head."

Laidlaw's co-worker Ted Backman echoes this reconstructionist sentiment in *Half-Life 2: Raising the Bar*. When designing the soldiers of the future, he decided they wouldn't need the shoulder pads every other videogame had them wearing: "I don't know if they think soldiers will be tackling people," he quips. Similarly, when designing monsters, he rethought the genre standbys: the Stalker "was a kind of nullified amputated human the Combine turned into a slave labourer ... that presented a moral dilemma every time you had to deal with it. It is more horrific to have to deal with an insane hostage than something that just wants to eat your brains."

Pirates of the Pacific

This past winter, Bruce and I took the trip out to Pacific Mall to get his PlayStation 2 modded. He was excited that he'd soon be able to play the pirated games he'd downloaded off the net, and I was excited about the amazing dim sum we'd be eating after. It was a pain getting to Kennedy and Steeles on transit in the snow, but had we waited till the spring Bruce would have been shit out of luck. The pirates have all now set sail.

Pacific Mall was as shiny and fabulous as I remembered, a piece of Hong Kong transplanted successfully into suburban Markham. We traipsed around to the various game stores, and Bruce would ask them questions about options and prices. They'd sometimes have price lists posted with different mod chips, preloaded packages and a catalogue of the bootleg games they had to offer.

After the third or fourth place offered the exact same price—$130 for the mod chip installation with three games, $110 with no games— Bruce started to grumble about honour among thieves. So he picked one that said they could do it in an hour, entrusting the two teenagers with the binder-sized console. The incongruity of the sleek tech coming out of his paint-flecked satchel gave it a spy-thriller feel.

I mentioned this as we sat down to lunch at Graceful Vegetarian Restaurant. "I think that's one of the reasons I like pirated games," Bruce said. "It's just more fun. Finding ways to get them rather than just going into a Wal-Mart—it becomes a game in itself. Unlike movies or music, videogames have always been digital—pirating games has been part of gaming culture from the beginning." He flipped over the menu. "Kind of expensive."

I assured him that once he tried the food his starving artist would be grateful. I called him on the fact that he was spending over a hundred bucks on a consumer purchase to avoid making consumer purchases.

"That's true," he said, "but once I saw the games available via bit torrent I decided it'd be worth it. I wouldn't have actually bought a PS2 at all if I couldn't get it modded—retail games are out of my budget. I'm not going to quit painting and get a crap job so I can buy a new game every month."

We ordered, checking off a bunch of tasties, and I asked him what the mod chip actually does. "Most games are just DVDs, right? So you should be able to just copy them like you do CDs. But they've got these unreproducable bad blocks on the original that DVD copying software corrects, then when you put the copy in the PS2 console, it looks for these bad blocks, and when it can't find them it refuses to play. The mod chip bypasses this bad-block-checking step."

Our food arrived and we ignored bad blocks in favour of good bok choy and a number of other amazing dishes that had Bruce converted and sated by the end of the meal. "Good value," he decided.

We returned to the store, where one of the young guys was hunched over another console, the guts open and tools applied. The other one showed us Bruce's console, plugged it into a couple of ready plugs and fired it up. The TV in the corner showed the familiar PlayStation logo boot-up screen with a small addendum in a corner reading "Infinity." A game booted up and Bruce nodded his approval, pulling out some cash. As he unplugged it, the guy explained that you wanted to keep the cover open while you played, to avoid overheating: the unit wasn't made to support another chip.

"Cool," Bruce said to me as we left. "It reminds me of a customized hot rod, with the engine exposed." He patted his bag happily. "That was easy. I sort of expected more cloak-and-dagger stuff."

As it turned out, the stores at Pacific Mall could have used a little more discretion. A few months after our trip, I got a press release: "The Entertainment Software Association (ESA) and the Entertainment Software Association of Canada (ESAC) joined today in applauding the Royal Canadian Mounted Police's (RCMP) recent actions against numerous retail outlets offering pirate and counterfeit entertainment software for sale at Pacific Mall in Markham, Ontario."

The release originated from Highroad, a PR company that represents Microsoft and often sends me information about Xbox titles, so I took them up on their offer to chat with Danielle LaBossiere, executive director of ESAC.

ESAC is a trade organization made up of most of the game companies that, according to Danielle, serves civil warnings—"kind of like cease-and-desist letters"—to people violating copyright law and then "work[s] very closely to keep [the RCMP] abreast [of these violations]." Then, in the case of the "fairly successful raid on Pacific Mall," they (and other trade organization representatives from the movie and music industries) go with the RCMP to identify the bootlegged games. In the case of the Pacific Mall's Fun Desk, a retailer that had already had a warning, they were shut down in early May. No arrests were made.

Danielle was a political staffer before she was hired in October, a one-person operation supported by various "researchers" and a US parent organization in Washington. "Piracy's a huge problem in Canada ... it discourages innovation." Danielle was particularly outraged that the manufacture of mod chips is not actually illegal in Canada, just the use of them to circumvent copy protection.

Out of curiosity, I called Fun Desk a little more than a week later to see if they were open. They were, so I asked them if they sold PlayStation 2 games.

"Yes," he said, adding hastily: "But only originals."

I expect it'll be a while before I get any vegetarian dim sum again.

INDEX

BIOS

Carol Borden is the comics editor and current evil overlord of the Cultural Gutter. You can read some of her writing on movies at the Toronto International Film Festival's Midnight Madness Blog and hear read some of her writing on the You Will Not Make It In Hollywood podcast. She lives in Michigan.

In addition to writing for the Cultural Gutter, **Ian Driscoll** is the screenwriter of numerous gutter-level features and short films including the Harry Knuckles series, Jesus Christ, Vampire Hunter, The Dead Sleep Easy and Smash Cut. He has also worked as a story editor on a number of feature films, and makes (mercifully infrequent) appearances in front of the camera. Ian has worked in advertising since 2000, and has acted as senior writer and/or creative director on numerous regional, national and international campaigns for both private and public sector clients. Since late 2008, he has been a partner in Ottawa's oldest surviving cinema, the Mayfair Theatre, which was recently voted Ottawa's "best alternative to a multiplex movie theatre."

Jim Munroe (b. 1972) is a "pop culture provocateur" according to the Austin Chronicle, and an "independent press icon" to Time Out Chicago. After leaving HarperCollins for political reasons, he founded No Media Kings and published five books, the most recent one a post-Rapture graphic novel called Therefore Repent! He also started The Perpetual Motion Roadshow, an indie touring circuit that sent 100 artists on the road between 2003-2007, and currently he is running the Artsy Games Incubator, a writer's-circle style group helping creators without programming skills make videogames. He lives in Toronto with a crafty ladyscientist and their bafflingly attractive baby.

James Schellenberg is a librarian, currently works in science outreach, and lives and writes in Ottawa. His website is at www.jschellenberg. com.

Chris Szego reads romance, mystery, SF&F, poetry, non-fiction of all kinds, children's books, newspapers, and things people leave on the subway (but not horror, because she's kind of a chicken). When not reading, writing or travelling, she manages Bakka-Phoenix, Canada's oldest SFF bookstore.